W9-BPJ-990

Steve —

Be on purpose!

The
KINGMAKER

A Leadership Story
of Integrity and Purpose

Tony Bridwell

Praise for

The KINGMAKER

"So many of us race through life striving to succeed and hoping to find a sense of purpose along the way. Tony Bridwell, in his book *The Kingmaker*, has an amazing ability to wake us up to the truths we have known for over 2,000 years. What we are called to do and how we live don't always match. *The Kingmaker* brings these lessons to life in a way I never will forget. I recommend this book to anyone with a pulse."

Wally Gomaa
MHA/MBA ACAP Health,
Chief Executive Officer

"Tony Bridwell, in *The Kingmaker*, has written a great leadership story that reminds us that leaders in search of achievement can lose their way. Our purpose should always be about making a difference in the lives of others."

Doug Brooks
Former CEO and COB of Brinker and
current member of the Board of Directors for
Southwest Airlines, AutoZone, and Club Corp.

"In *The Kingmaker*, Tony Bridwell does an incredible job making a case for purpose over profits through the lives of four kings, and their maker. The characters and their struggles are relatable to anyone in business and the lessons are thoughtful and profound. In the end, and as it should be – those who truly live their purpose always find their way. A fantastic read."

Kelli Valade,
EVP COO Chili's,
Brinker International

"Tony Bridwell has written a compelling story that should be carefully read by anyone aspiring to leadership and, especially, by those who are "leaders of leaders." I read *The Kingmaker* twice – once for the story and then again to solidify my understanding of the principles Tony drives toward."

Tom Miller,
President Symbolist,
Author of *Lift*

"In *The Kingmaker*, Tony Bridwell reveals two distinct paths in life: one where our efforts change the world around us for the better and one where our short-term gains bring long-term dissatisfaction and heartache. The choice is ours."

Craig Hickman
New York Times Bestselling Author of
The Insiders and *Mind of a Manager Soul of a Leader*

"The great challenge for any leader is crafting a meaningful and motivating purpose for their time on earth. In *The Kingmaker*, Tony Bridwell creates a captivating story of the importance of that purpose being rooted in servant-leadership and unlocking the greatest potential in others."

John Luke Spitler
President/CEO,
Encompass Staffing Inc. and The Encompass Group

"Today, as people are seeking greater significance in their lives, Tony Bridwell reminds us in *The Kingmaker* that you have the power to transform your legacy through simple changes in your philosophy. I strongly encourage you to read this book and chart your course for the future."

Dr. Brent Taylor
Pastor of First Baptist Church Carrollton and
Author of *Founding Leadership: Lessons on Business and Personal Leadership From the Men Who Brought You the American Revolution*

"Tony Bridwell's *The Kingmaker* reminds me that at the essence of leadership is the purpose of serving others and that the positive, purposeful, and high-integrity leaders will always win the race in the end."

Patrick Droesch
EVP, Club Corp.,
Business Sports & Alumni Division

"In the business parable, *The Kingmaker*, author Tony Bridwell brilliantly tells the story of a group of wealthy and powerful clients, friends and colleagues who ultimately must face gut-wrenching decisions about their careers, marriages, and legacies based on how they choose to define "success." Spoiler alert: You will be a better person, and the world will be a better place if you embrace the powerful wisdom of the *The Kingmaker.*"

Joni Thomas Doolin
CEO & Founder,
TDn2k & People Report

"I often reflect on the messaging I am sending my team and the legacy I am creating. In *The Kingmaker*, Tony Bridwell reminds us that positively changing our legacy can be accomplished by a simple change of philosophy."

Edie Ames
President,
The Counter Burger

"*The Kingmaker* by Tony Bridwell is one of the most thoughtful and insightful pieces of work I have ever read. It truly gets the reader to think about who they are as leaders and perhaps even more importantly, what they want to become. A must-read for anyone who is a perpetual learner!"

David Nosal
Chairman and Managing Partner,
NGS Global

"Tony Bridwell has done it again. Brilliantly! In *The Kingmaker*, we are reminded that, being human, we can lose focus and end up in a place we never intended to visit—or stay. If we are aware and associate with loved ones and friends who care about us, we can choose the path that will take us back to servant-centered leadership. Or not. Bridwell shows us that the choice is ours."

Leon Kaplan
CEO/President,
ABCO International

"Through *The Kingmaker*, Tony Bridwell provides a view into what it looks like to live with purpose, to truly live in service of others. His characters struggle like all of us. This thought-provoking book is worth the investment in time and ultimately contemplation."

Chris Willis
CHRO and General Counsel
Interstate Batteries

The

KINGMAKER

A Leadership Story
of Integrity and Purpose

Editorial Work: Anna McHargue

Cover Design: Aaron Snethen

Interior Design: Aaron Snethen

Portrait Photography: Morgan Chidsey, A SEA OF LOVE Photography

This book may be purchased in bulk for educational, business, organizational or
promotional use. To do so, contact Elevate Publishing at info@elevatepub.com

ISBN Book: 9781943425303

ISBN eBook: 9781943425648

Library Of Congress: 2015956311

Dedication

To my one True KING and to Dee,
my bride of 25 years

THE KINGMAKER

The door to the historic building opened on cue as the doorman anticipated Kyle's stride. Once outside the building, a quick
glance up and down Central Park West gave the all-clear and
Kyle's pace quickened. The early morning air offered a moist
softness as he glided through the streetlight-lit street. The City
was never completely dark even at this hour of the morning. A
cut-through at 69th Street, a short half-block sprint, and Kyle
was quickly and effortlessly on West Drive in Central Park for his
head-clearing run.

On a Sunday morning the park was a special type of quiet. Giv-
en the park was never really without people, Kyle had learned
over the years that 5:30 a.m. was the best time to avoid the two-
wheel demon road bikers out to set land speed records. Only the
most serious runners could be spotted in the pre-dawn glow of
the streetlights. The otherwise present tourists were still sleeping
off their previous night's activities, freeing his path from unwant-
ed distractions.

The road was clear, the air just warm enough to generate a
cleansing bead of sweat. For the next 60 minutes there would
be no disruptions. The time alone was much needed given the
events of the last several days concerning those he cared for the
most. The Bose headphones were Bluetoothed to his ever-pres-

ent smart phone playing his favorite running playlist. It seemed today, the music was simply white noise as Kyle's mind played through all that had unfolded.

Out of habit he glanced to check his heart rate as he approached the first subtle hill in the park. Even the added stress from an elite group of clients, combined with an unusually brisk pace that morning, had only moved his heart to 136 bpm. At 52, Kyle's attention to his health was known by all close to him, especially his bride, Em, better known around the City as Emily.

It wasn't out of the ordinary to have Em join him for his Sunday morning run through the Park in the early days of their marriage, or afterward for a café latte at Joe's, before heading off to church. Lunch in the Park and a stroll back to their West Side penthouse capped a typical Sunday. Those typical days had past.

Today Kyle found himself in the situation he dreaded most, running alone.

After 15 minutes Kyle's mind was fully engulfed with the details of what his driver Mac had referred to as *The Collapse*. Mac always had a way of getting to the point. After so many years together there was no one Kyle trusted more, outside of Em, than Mac. To call him just a driver was selling him short. Kyle and Mac's friendship stretched back to grad school and was forged in the crucible of great stress and controversy.

Having been raised in an affluent family, Mac, or Parker Macintosh II as he was formally named, struggled his entire life to gain his father's respect. His father was a self-made millionaire owning several businesses along the East Coast. Mac's lifelong obsession to please his father led him down a path of Ivy undergrad and a Master's in Psychology—earned in the hopes of better understanding his father. Ultimately, his quest led him to a Ph.D. in Anthropology, which he believed could gain his father's respect. It was during his time at Columbia that Kyle and Mac first crossed paths.

The six-foot tall Mac started to go bald while still in school. Now he simply wore a slick shaved head that was rarely without semi-round, black-rimmed glasses. Black jeans, lightly starched white shirt, and a custom-made jacket, designed to conceal his licensed weapon of choice, finished his look. Today, the weapon of choice was Mac's favorite Kimber .45, a gift from a group of Navy Seals he had spent time mentoring after their return from active duty.

At 54 Mac's ability to read people had been honed to perfection. His attention to his health and fitness was the only activity that surpassed his passion for observing people. In fact, it was his thirst to learn more about people that led him to take on the challenge of Doctoral work in Anthropology. Mac's first encounter with Kyle occurred while teaching a class on Commerce and the Human Virtue. Over the course of the semester, their friendship began to build as Kyle recognized the true intellect built into the semi-geeky frame that was the early version of Parker Macintosh.

As Mac prepared to present his dissertation, life took an unexpected turn. Within Mac's doctoral cohort existed one student focused on doing anything and everything necessary to complete his dissertation. As it turned out not only did the student violate the university's Code of Conduct but also, in an effort to cover his tracks, framed Mac for plagiarism and theft.

The scandal rocked the school. Within days the scandal had wreaked havoc on Mac's life, costing him his job, his girlfriend, and, ultimately, his degree. The speed in which the entire event happened caught most people – including Kyle – by surprise. By the time Kyle wrapped his head around what was happening, the damage had been done and justice had been lost.

Mac would say it was at this moment in Kyle's life that Kyle realized his true giftedness. Mobilizing his network of friends Kyle was able to bring the real culprit to justice and clear Mac's name. The genius of what Kyle accomplished was his masterful ability to facilitate – some might say manipulate – people to a required outcome. Effortlessly, like a grand master in chess, Kyle crafted a network of people, who individually appeared to be innocuous, but while working together in concert created a deadly assault on their intended victim.

Having his name cleared meant more to Mac than the paper that would hang on the wall declaring him a Ph.D. in Anthropology. His allegiance to Kyle had been sealed. In a twist of role reversal, Mac offered himself to Kyle as his personal driver and security. The protected became the protector. Through the years Mac's loyalty had given him an insider's vantage point to Kyle's dealings with the most influential people in the world.

To the outside world Mac's boss was known simply as Kyle Ellis, CEO of ELLIS, a boutique international public relations consulting company. With billings close to $100 million annually, ELLIS was ranked in the top five of all PR firms in the world. To an outsider needing a public relations partner, the ELLIS organization was well known for its efficient and effective work. What the outside world did not know was that ELLIS was much more than a PR firm . . . the organization had a true specialty: bringing people to the top. To an elite circle of people in the world, Kyle Ellis was, in fact, known as The Kingmaker.

THE COLLAPSE

The text message required a second glance. Kyle slowly scrolled through the message carefully reading each word. *"Heads up. Kit on front page of* WSJ *in 24."* The message, from a trusted friend inside the *Journal*, could only mean one thing: trouble.

"Mac, change of plans. Head downtown to Kit's place." Mac knew immediately that something was up. Kyle rarely changed his morning routine. The drive to One World Trade Center gave Kyle just enough time to send a follow-up text to his trusted friend, Kim, at the *Journal*.

Kyle: *"What should I know?"*

Kim: *"Scandal."*

Kyle: *"Serious or superficial?"*

Kim: *"Serious."*

Kyle: *"TY."*

As Mac was pulling into the garage of the new glistening tower, Kyle sent a text to Kit's assistant.

Kyle: *"On my way up, clear his schedule."*

The express elevator ride up the 81 floors was an ear-popping quick ride. In a matter of a few minutes, Kyle was stepping into the private lobby of SnyderPerkins, one of Wall Street's most powerful financial institutions. At 38, Kit Jackson was the firm's youngest CEO in its storied 65-year history. The media always had had a love affair with Kit. Standing six-foot, one inch tall with piercing blue eyes and thick black hair, Kit had a prep school boyish face, which the camera loved. His youthful appearance had caused the demise of those who underestimated him.

Being heavily recruited in high school to play Division I football by most of the SEC, Kit learned early in his adult life that he could have anything he wanted simply by asking. Over time, though, just asking wasn't enough. Kit further developed his skills of acquiring what he wanted through a combination of his looks and his talent. During his time at Harvard while completing his MBA, Kit heard rumors of The Kingmaker as someone who could be of benefit to Kit's eager desire to conquer all that he saw in his path.

During his first year as a junior associate for SnyderPerkins, Kit became restless. Spending his time sizing up the other associates as if they were an enemy to be slain, Kit obsessed over how he might obtain the top job. One by one he plotted against anyone willing to get into his way. While this strategy initially proved successful, the bridges he was burning along the way began to slow his advancement considerably. Once he reached the vice president level, that advancement reached an abrupt halt. It was at this point he remembered all that he had heard of The Kingmaker.

Using his NCAA connections as well as the few friends he had remaining, Kit was able to track down The Kingmaker's identity. After a few weeks of planning, Kit found his opportunity to connect with Kyle during a SnyderPerkins charity event at Lincoln Center. Normally, Kyle would not spend time at events such as these, but this one, which benefited the American Heart Association, was different. Emily's father had passed away from heart disease when she was only 12. As an adult her passion has been to find a cure. If it was Em's passion, it was Kyle's passion.

The first encounter between Kit and Kyle was well rehearsed on Kit's part. Knowing he might only get one shot at working with Kyle, he had to be on his game. Kit's plan was to leverage the thin relationships remaining within the firm to score an invite to the private VIP reception held in the Hauser Patron Salon overlooking West 65th Street. Once inside the reception he would be free to target Kyle in the intimate settings of the salon.

In fewer than seven years, following Kyle's well-orchestrated plan, Kit soon found himself not only leading the powerhouse of

Wall Street but also marrying the co-founder's granddaughter. Sara Perkins was a former international runway model when she and Kit were first introduced. To assure Kit's rise to the top, Kyle orchestrated the meeting between Kit and Sara as a way to move Kit into the family side of the business. Sara's striking beauty was unequaled. The minute Kit shared a private moment with her he knew then he wanted her by his side.

After five years as CEO Kit's accomplishments proved his worth as a leader and shifted the murmured rumors of his position being a family gift. Kit, for all his faults, knew how to make money for his investors, his firm, and especially himself. Kit also knew with money came power, which he used freely to get what he wanted, no matter the cost.

The last time Kit was mentioned in the *WSJ* was when the paper ran its annual report on the highest paid executives in the nation. Kit ranked in the top five at $120 million for the year. With a net worth of well over $1.2 billion, Kit was well-entrenched into an exceptional circle of "friends," a term loosely applied within the City. Whenever the City's leading power couple hosted a fundraiser for the Arts in their Upper East Side penthouse, the news was sure to find its way onto Page Six as a social event of the season. By all measures Kit had found the top of the success ladder. Even with all the money, success, and power, though, Kit once again found he needed the help of the man who put him on top.

Kit Jackson's office had a panoramic view of the City. As Kyle entered the space he found Kit standing inches away from the floor-to-ceiling glass, staring into the vast sea of high-rise buildings, looking north and east. From the 81st floor the view was remarkable. The day was clear and Kit had fixed his gaze on the Empire State Building in the distance. Kyle stood quietly knowing Kit sensed his presence.

"A majestic masterpiece, isn't she?" were the first words out of Kit's mouth.

"Which one?" responded Kyle.

"The Empire." "She has stood the test of time . . . a true masterpiece." Kit's voice trailed off a bit as he turned to face Kyle for the first time.

"I suppose you're correct, she has stood the test of time since she first opened her doors in 1931," said Kyle. "It's amazing what you can stand when you are built on a solid foundation," he added.

Kit's eyes told most of the story for Kyle. "I was planning to call you later today once I confirmed the story was going to run."

"It seems your sources are better than mine in this case," Kit said with a hint of distain. Kyle, sensing the shifting tone in Kit's voice, allowed the comment to pass.

"What's going on, Kit?"

"It's simple, the *Journal* is trying to sell papers and I happen to be a handy billionaire to pick on this month," rattled Kit, his tone of voice strong but uneven. "It is just a bunch of BS. Some rookie beat reporter has convinced the editor there is a story."

Knowing Kit all too well, Kyle could see right through the anemic attempt to conceal the truth. "Sounds easy enough to fix. You can sue the paper for slander and have it retracted. I know a great lawyer," Kyle offered. Kit's silence spoke louder than words. His gaze faded downward and away from Kyle and back to the expansive glass wall.

After a moment of time, Kit spoke, "No need for any lawyers, I have a dozen on retainer. Truth is, Kyle, the story has legs, weak legs, but legs."

Kyle measured his response carefully. "You want to tell me about it?"

"The paper will claim I conspired to ruin Howard Payne and his business through a series of stock manipulation schemes. The SEC will be the next call I receive after the story runs if they haven't been tipped off already," Kit confessed.

The relationship between Kit and Howard went back several years, the two always admiring each other's work. Howard

Payne, most would tell you, was Kit Jackson's last real friend. The friend body count over the years had grown steadily higher for Kit. He systematically destroyed every single relationship he had ever forged – with the exception of two: his wife Sara and Howard Payne. For this story to be true, the unthinkable had occurred.

Still staring out the window Kit remarked, "I am not sorry for what I did; I am sorry it appears I have been found out. You have fixed bigger issues than this in the past, old friend. Now it's time to fix this one."

As one of the leading crisis management firms in the world, EL-LIS was the company you wanted handling your response when stories such as this made their way above the fold on the front page of the *WSJ*. Knowing what was at stake, Kyle sent a text message to his assistant to ready a crisis team to handle the details. A second text was sent to Mac, *"Heading down with Kit. Having lunch at office. Order up usual for both."*

"First things, first, Kit. I need to get you to neutral ground. You are having lunch with me back at the shop. Mac is downstairs," Kyle said. Kit had learned over time not to argue with Kyle when a certain tone surfaced in his voice. For the first time in several years, Kit realized the intention behind Kyle's tone and had but one response, "I will get my bag."

The 20-minute trip uptown to Kyle's office in the historic Fuller Building allowed Kyle the opportunity to probe Kit for clarity. "Last I heard, Howard was your last-standing friend," Kyle said, breaking the silence that had filled the car for the last 10 blocks.

"Friends are overrated," responded Kit as he stared out the tinted window of the Mercedes S600 sedan.

"I wish your response was more shocking, but it seems I have come to expect that from you," replied Kyle.

"Hey, this is tough business and you know it. Either you move first or you get run over. Don't play the naïve kid from Texas with me," Kit replied in a biting tone.

With practiced ease, Mac maneuvered the sedan into the private parking space. Within moments the art deco elevator doors opened and the three men began their journey to Kyle's office. The lobby space on the 17th floor was the entryway to ELLIS' New York headquarters. Kyle's office took much of the northeast corner of the building and, for now, still allowed him a small view of Central Park.

Updates on the pending article began streaming in the moment they entered Kyle's office. Kyle scanned down a printed copy of tomorrow's article acquired after several phone calls to key sources within the *WSJ*. The article, a 2,000-word introduction for what the author and the paper hoped would be a multiple-week scandal of epic proportions. Midway through reading, Kyle's face began to tighten. The story being told about Kit, even if half true, was horrific.

Kyle turned to Kit, who had made his way to the overstuffed couch. "Kit, I need the truth. What did Howard have that you wanted?" Kyle inquired. But Kyle knew Kit well enough to discern the real reason the story had legs. While the reporter's allegations might have been close and a case could be made in the court of public opinion, there was much more to this story and Kyle knew it.

"I don't know what you mean," responded Kit, as he sipped a double espresso.

"You darn well know what I mean. I've seen this before in you. When you want something, there is little you won't do to get it. Now, what did Howard have that you wanted and was worth ruining your only friend for?" said Kyle.

"Like I said Kyle, friends are overrated," retorted Kit.

As Kyle was preparing to press Kit further, Mac entered the room. "Boss, something you need to see," Mac quietly offered. Kyle's trust in Mac told him only something of the utmost importance would ever have Mac interrupt a conversation. Kyle excused himself from Kit and stepped into the outer office area connecting his office with the open concept area that made up the bulk of the floor.

"What is it, Mac?"

Mac handed Kyle his cell phone while offering a brief explanation, "Just got this text from one of my Navy Seal buddies working a security detail for Michael Allen."

"Credible threat to MA's company and his life. Need to give KE heads up."

"How good is your buddy?" asked Kyle still looking at the text.

"He will keep Michael safe, for now. I just spoke with him and it seems Michael may have pushed a deal too far with the wrong people," Mac offered.

"Sounds more like a job for the NYPD than me. Why the heads up?" asked Kyle.

"The threat to his life was bigger than just taking him out. The threat was total destruction of Prime Networks after killing both Michael and his family first."

Kyle let the words settle in for a brief moment before he responded, "Michael has always pushed the envelope on his deals, but in the last 10 years nothing has reached this level of response. Who is he trying to take over?" asked Kyle.

"Small group, maybe half-a-billion deal. Strong rumors that there are Russian mob connections," Mac added.

"What the heck has Michael gotten himself into this time?" Kyle wondered out loud with Mac. "Find out where he is right now so I can speak with him," Kyle asked.

"On it!" responded Mac as he peeled away from where they were standing.

As Mac was walking away, Kyle stopped him to ask, "Mac, have all of our Kings gone crazy at once?"

Mac turned toward Kyle with a slight grin and replied, "It does appear to be a collapse. I believe there is a common thread; we can talk later."

THE FRIEND

Kit was midway through his lunch when Kyle entered the room. Sitting at the large conference table that resembled a reclaimed dinner table, Kit never looked up from his meal as Kyle took the seat opposite. Unfolding his neatly pressed napkin, Kyle surveyed his meal. Quality Italian Steakhouse had become a favorite of Kyle's from the moment they opened their doors on 57th Street just blocks away from the office. As Kyle forked the first bite of his seared yellowfin tuna salad, his mind raced in multiple directions playing each possible scenario of not only Kit's current challenge but now Michael's threat to his business and his life. Knowing Kit's narcissism and having a personal policy of never discussing clients with clients, Kyle jumped straight to the pressing point at hand. "The team is finalizing the communication plan to go out tomorrow," Kyle said. "We began working this story the moment we received the tip and have an aggressive strategy to move this from a front page scandal to a back page non-story within the week."

Kit finally looked up from his plate and responded," I had no doubt you could handle this. Just one thing, why am I here? We could have done this at my office."

Kyle responded back without missing a beat, "Frankly Kit, I can't trust you to stay out of further trouble so I need to keep an eye on you." Kit's eye roll in response to Kyle's remark was heard loudly.

"Kit, I need you to level with me if we are going to be sure this stays off of the front page," Kyle offered. By now Kit had finished his lunch and was up walking around the expansive office. Settling down in the seating area, which was surrounded on three sides by library book stacks reaching the top of the 12-foot ceiling, Kit crossed one leg over the other and sat fixing his gaze on Kyle.

After a few moments of silence, Kit finally spoke, "When was the last time you saw Howard?"

"It was late last year at the SoHo art gallery reception. Why?" replied Kyle. At that moment Mac slipped up behind Kyle leaning close in to quietly relay a message.

"Security team just disarmed an explosive device in one of Michael's vehicles. Michael and family are okay, just shaken by the news. Authorities have been notified."

Kyle turned his head away from Kit's view and softly responded to Mac, "Where is he now?"

Having anticipated the question, Mac responded, "En route to the ranch."

Kyle nodded in approval, knowing Michael's 25,000-acre ranch, The Lazy Deuce, in Wyoming was the safest place for him at this point. "Call the hanger and have the plane made ready, wheels up by 6:00," Kyle added. As smoothly as he had entered, Mac retreated to prepare for their trip to see Michael.

Kit naturally thought the added distractions were only due to his current needs. "How long do I need to stay here, old friend?" asked Kit.

"Our team should have your team briefed and will go over your talking points in a few minutes," replied Kyle. "We will get through this, Kit, but my gut tells me something else is brewing, and if you aren't going to be completely honest, you are putting both of us in a weakened position," Kyle added.

Kit rose from the couch and walked toward Kyle. "We will be fine; just get this whole matter off the front page and all will be good," Kit said.

"My Chief-of-Staff will review talking points with you. Listen to her and do not deviate from our plan. You and Sara should plan on dinner at home tonight to avoid some hired-gun paparazzi looking to score a front page surprise shot," Kyle said with added sternness. "My office has been working with yours to clear your calendar and keep you out of harm's way for the next week or so. It will be best for you to remain in the City doing some low-profile events that we can control in an effort to not appear as though we are running away from the story. We have a contact at The New Yorker ready to run a fluff piece extolling your amazing contributions to the City. That one will cost us," Kyle confessed.

Kit smiled gently, taking in all that was happening in front of him. In a just a few hours Kyle and his team had masterfully planned a media escape route to safety in effortless fashion. "You are worth every dollar I have paid you over the years," Kit said with what seemed to be a genuine tone in his voice.

"Thank you, Kit, but we are not out of this yet," responded Kyle.

"It is clear you have everything under control. Can I go home now?" asked Kit.

"Your car is on its way and has been given instructions to take you home," Kyle said. Kit smiled, knowing that Kyle was serious and any override of his instructions would not be worth the wrath that would follow. "Yes, sir," Kit said with a hint of sarcasm.

Kit walked over and took a last sip of his post-lunch drink, grabbed his bag, and headed for the door having been alerted his driver was waiting in the garage. As he approached the door,

Kyle inquired one more time, "Why Howard, Kit?" With his hand on the door never turning toward Kyle he responded, "I really like Howard. Heck, at the end of the day, everyone likes Howard." With that Kit walked out the door and toward the private entrance to the elevator.

THE FLIGHT

Kyle tapped "send" on the text to Em. *Heading to The Lazy Deuce for last-minute dinner with MA. Back for dinner tomorrow, me and you at the steakhouse.*

Over the years Emily had never fully adjusted to the last-minute changes to their plans. What struck her as odd in this case was Michael's current wife had become semi-close with Emily. Having been married four times over the last 20 years, it had been difficult to get close to any of Michael's previous wives, but Mackenzie was different. After enjoying several extended girl weekends at The Lazy Deuce, Emily was surprised she was not invited along for Kyle's trip to see Michael.

"Is Kenz at the ranch?"

"Yes"

"Would love to catch up with her. Have room for one more?"

The last text from Emily was purely rhetorical given Kyle's Gulf-stream G280 was fitted to carry eight and sleep four.

"Not a good time this trip but will plan one soon."

"Be safe."

Kyle looked up from his phone and confided in Mac, "Em wants to go, but I am uncomfortable given the safety issue."

Mac gave Kyle a nod of approval but wondered if the pending safety concerns really were the only reason Em hadn't been included. It had becoming increasingly obvious to Mac that the two people he cared for the most had been silently slipping apart. Mac had promised himself not to intervene unless asked by either Kyle or Emily. Until now they had chosen to suffer alone. "I told her we would be back in time for dinner tomorrow, at the steakhouse," Kyle said.

"I checked the weather; we should be good. I'll make reservations once we get to the hanger," Mac assured Kyle.

The 40-minute drive to Teterboro Airport gave Kyle time to do some pre-flight preparations. Both Kyle and Mac had shared the love of flying since their college years and did their best thinking while piloting. ELLIS had a full-time pilot on staff ready to take Kyle and the team anywhere needed in any one of his three planes. The G280 was by far his favorite. With a top speed of

560 mph and a range of 4,100 miles, there were few places Kyle could not get to with ease.

"Looks like we are just under four hours once wheels up if the winds hold," Kyle reported to Mac. "A few storms to our south that we will want to watch, but we should be good given our speed," Kyle added. "The slowest part will be passing over Chicago. Dang traffic coming into that city is ridiculous."

Kyle loved to fly. It was one of the few places he could gather his thoughts. Spending time in the air with Mac over the years had proved to be some of their most impactful time together. As Mac said, it is hard to get distracted at 45,000 feet.

Pulling into the private hanger Mac parked the car to one side of the aircraft. Opening the trunk revealed two overnight bags that Mac kept on hand for times just as this. The crew gave Mac the final paperwork and a quick debrief on the current traffic in and out of the airport. As a reliever airport for the City, traffic in and out of Teterboro was high volume for an airport its size.

As Mac climbed the steps into KE4686, the tail number for the Gulfstream and also Kyle and Emily's wedding anniversary, he stowed the bags in the front galley and climbed into the right seat to begin his pre-flight checklist. Kyle was midway around the plane's exterior doing his customary visual inspection when the text message tone on his cell alerted him to an incoming message.

"Going to miss you tonight, be safe. Tell Mac I said Hi...Love you."

The note from Em created a tightening in Kyle's chest as he read. He knew deep inside that their relationship had not been as good as it used to be in the early years. It seemed life had gradually picked up pace, and with each new client, there was less and less time for Emily.

"Love you, too, Em. See you for dinner," Kyle typed into the message box on his phone. He stood for a moment with his finger hovering over the send button as he contemplated the words he'd just typed. They were easy to type, but for some reason they felt so very hollow. With a tap Kyle sent the message, knowing Emily would give anything to have the words of his message to be true.

Kyle finished his check and climbed into the left pilot seat and wrapped the headset around his neck, checking the instrument panel verifying the heading for the flight.

Mac said, "Ready to run through the check?"

"Let's go," replied Kyle as he adjusted his headset. Within a few minutes the two were ready to be towed out of the hanger and to the taxiway to get in line for departure.

Kyle pressed the button for his headset, "Tower, this is Kilo Echo 4686 on taxiway, requesting departure runway 24 with right turn." "Roger that, Kilo Echo 4686. You are clear for departure behind November Papa 9515 for runway 24 with right turn. Light winds from the southwest with clear visibility at 10 miles, heavy traffic in the area, go to 10,000 feet after right turn and hold for five miles," commanded the tower to Kyle. "Roger that, tower, coming in behind November Papa 9515 for departure runway 24 with right turn, light winds out of southwest with clear visibility at 10 miles, will go to 10,000 feet after right turn and hold for five miles. Thanks for the help."

Kyle eased the plane into position while double-checking his settings one last time. Mac pulled on his seatbelt to ensure the tightness was appropriate for the upcoming burst of speed. "Tower, this is Kilo Echo 4686 ready on 24," Kyle informed the tower.

"Kilo Echo 4686, you are clear runway 24. Enjoy your flight," the tower responded. "Roger that, tower. Kilo Echo 4686 out." And with those words from Kyle, the 67-foot-long plane began its journey down the 6,013 feet of runway 24, only needing just over 4,700 feet before the powerful engines lifted the Gulfstream effortlessly into the air.

Even after a thousand or more departures, Kyle's heart rate quickened when he felt the thrust of the engines and his body being pulled back into his well-padded captain's seat. Gently, Kyle banked right and climbed to 10,000 feet as instructed by the tower. The City quickly disappeared as KE4686 increased her speed in route to The Lazy Deuce ranch.

Once they reached 10,000 feet, Kyle heard from the tower, "Kilo Echo 4686, hold 10,000 for five miles then climb to 40,000."

Kyle responded, "Roger that, tower, hold at 10,000 for five miles then climb to 40,000. Kilo Echo 4686 out."

Within moments Kyle and Mac were at cruising altitude and clear of much of the heavy traffic around the tri-state area. Once at 40,000 feet, Mac spoke into his voice-activated headset, "Perfect night for a flight."

"Haven't seen flying weather like this in a couple months; should be a quick flight," Kyle responded.

Once the last checks were made, Mac eased his seat back and let Kyle know he would start some coffee. The Gulfstream, on autopilot, offered Kyle a chance to unwind. "That sounds like a plan," Kyle announced over the headset. Within moments the bright lights that had created an amber glow on the horizon began to diminish as the jet made its way into the western region of Pennsylvania. Mac returned shortly to produce two brewed cups of freshly ground coffee. The slight smile on Kyle's face was all the thanks needed. Mac slid into the right seat and buckled back into place.

"Nothing like a fresh-brewed cup of coffee," Kyle announced.

Mac's agreement was mid sip, "Umm."

"Help me sort through the craziness, Mac. What in the world is going on these days?" Kyle began. "You said you had a theory. I am all ears," he continued.

After a few additional sips of coffee, Mac responded, "We will know more once we land and get some answers, but I do have some observations. If you think about it not all of your clients are in a tailspin. The collapse has exposed two very high-profile clients, but let's look at two clients still in thriving mode. Take for example Kevin Westfield and Clara Becker."

Over the years, Kyle had been grateful for the depth of Mac's wisdom. One of Mac's many gifts was his ability to slow Kyle's thinking so that he had a chance to see a bigger picture. The examples of Kevin and Clara were perfect examples of clients making a positive difference in the world.

Kevin Westfield was CEO of McDaniel Exploration, the second largest privately held oil and gas company in the world. Kyle first met Kevin while in grad school. Their friendship would have been classified as casual in the early days. But over the next few years post-Columbia, they easily remained in touch given both stayed in the City and found themselves living in the same building for a period of time.

Kyle spoke into his headset softly, "Mac, I remember a conversation with Kevin after grad school like it was yesterday." Kyle continued, "I went for a run one morning and encountered Kevin when I got home."

"Hey, Kyle, great morning for a run. How far today?" Kevin asked while propping the door open for Kyle to enter.

"Hey, Kevin, hello. Just a quick five miles. Promised Em brunch this morning. Where are you heading off to this early hour?" Kyle asked with a bit of nosey curiosity.

"Heading downtown to meet a girl at church." "Hold the presses!" exclaimed Kyle. "A girl? This seems like a new development. I realize we haven't seen each other in like a week. So, tell me, what's the story?" Kyle poked for answers.

Kevin stepped out of the door and onto the sidewalk to answer Kyle. He was aglow with a smile that covered his face. "Her name is Lindsey, but her friends call her Chase," Kevin began.

"Question is what do you call her?" Kyle asked with a slight grin on his face.

Kevin replied with a slight grin of his own. "She is really sweet. We met through a mutual friend of ours last week. Only been on one date but have it bad for her. She could be the one, Kyle." Kevin's face was beginning to flush with excitement. "She said if I wanted to see her today, I could meet her at church and grab a bite afterwards. Kyle, I haven't been in a church since high school. Not sure I remember how to act," Kevin confessed with real nervousness in his voice.

"You will be fine," Kyle offered as comfort as he grabbed the handle of the door to make his exit.

"Thanks, Kyle. I wanted to let you know I got the job with the oil and gas company out of Houston. It was my second choice, but a job is a job. They want me to start in 30 days."

Kyle's grin was a bit more forced now as he responded, "That is great news. How does Lindsey feel about Houston?"

It was obvious from Kevin's reaction he had not made the connection between the two situations. Seeing the devastation on Kevin's face Kyle's first thought was to try and soften the blow of the revelation now facing his friend. "Hey, I am sure it will be fine. Let's grab some breakfast tomorrow and we can talk through this some more. "City Diner on 90th, 7:30," Kyle offered.

Still a bit stunned by his miscalculation, Kevin nodded with a weak response, "Thanks, Kyle. You are a decent friend. See you in the morning."

Kyle pulled the door to their building opened and turned to Kevin to offer one last word of encouragement, "Enjoy church; it will do you good." And with that, he watched Kevin step to the sidewalk to hail a cab.

"I remember this story from the early years of the firm," Mac replied. "How did breakfast turn out the next day?" Kyle slid his seat back and unbuckled his harness then announced, "That was an interesting breakfast, but we are going to need more coffee to get through that one." "Roger that, Captain," was the response from Mac.

Kyle reappeared in a few moments with fresh coffee in both hands. "Sleep doesn't seem likely tonight so might as well enjoy," quipped Kyle as he effortlessly slid back into his seat. "So, you were telling the story about breakfast with Kevin," Mac reminded Kyle as he sipped his coffee.

Kyle began, "Breakfast the next day was not what I expected it to be."

Mac was quick to ask, "How do you mean?"

"What I thought was going to be a conversation about the new job turned out to be something entirely different," Kyle replied.

"But wasn't the breakfast the genesis of you working with Kevin?" Mac asked.

Kyle paused before responding, "It was, just didn't go as I thought it would."

Kyle had habit of arriving early for meetings. After years of playing competitive sports, he'd learned quickly that being late to a meeting was not acceptable if you were going to play in the big leagues. That day it was no different. Kyle walked into the City Diner at 7:10 a.m. only to find Kevin nursing a cup of black coffee. Kyle walked up to the table without Kevin noticing and pulled out the chair. "Good morning. Didn't expect to see you here this early," Kyle announced in a rather upbeat fashion for the early hour.

Kevin's coffee cup trance was broken in an instant. He looked up, offered a grin, extended his hand and responded, "Great to see you. Thanks for showing up."

Within seconds, Alexi, a 70-year-old New Yorker from the Bronx, showed up extending a cup in one hand and a pot of coffee in the other. "Mornin' Sweetheart, the usual?" she blurted out with an energy that was heard throughout the entire diner. Everyone was Sweetheart to Alexi, mostly because her memory was beginning to slip and names were harder to remember. After four decades of serving coffee at the City Diner, she had become a legend around this part of the City.

"Good morning to you Miss Alexi. Yes, please, the usual for me. My friend is new here. What would you recommend for him this morning?" Kyle said with a hint of flirting in his voice. Alexi's face began to glow, her body language beginning to show a bit of attitude as she lingered tableside. Alexi never lingered. Looking straight into Kevin's eyes she proclaimed, "You should have what this sweetheart is having. You can trust Kyle's judgment on many things, food being the top of the list." With that Kevin sat up taller in his chair and with a bit of renewed energy responded, "Thanks Alexi, I will have what he is having."

As quickly as she appeared, she disappeared to behind the counter to shout out the order in her well-refined Brooklyn accent. With one seamless motion, she grabbed three plates that were waiting in the pass-through window, stacked them up her arm, then grabbed a fourth plate and headed back to the tables. Her pace was constant, her smile as well as her uniquely New York attitude, always obvious.

Kevin leaned across the table holding his coffee with both hands and said to Kyle, "Alexi seems to really like her job."

Kyle smiled, took a long sip of coffee and responded, "Not sure she would call it a job; it's more like a passion for her. It is her fuel that keeps her going. I am not sure how long she would last if she wasn't doing this." Kyle continued, "She once joked to me that she wished she was more stable given this was her fourth job." They both laughed simultaneously at the thought.

After the laughter settled Kyle inquired, "So, how was your day with Lindsey?" Before Kevin could answer Alexi appeared out of nowhere with plates in both hands. "Here you go, Sweetheart, enjoy," Alexi proclaimed as she slid the plates onto the table. From the front pocket of the apron that bore her name, she produced a bottle of ketchup and hot sauce, anticipating Kyle's next request before he was able to get the words out. "Anything else, just holler."

Kevin carefully examined what he had ordered before answering Kyle. "Our day was amazing. With the exception of our time in church, we didn't stop talking," Kevin explained as he forked into his egg white omelet.

"Did you bring up Houston?" Kyle asked.

"Kinda," Kevin responded not looking up while answering.

Kyle chuckled a bit, "What does, kinda, mean?"

"Well, I asked her if she had ever been to Texas."

Kyle paused from eating and stared at Kevin for a brief moment before responding, "That is one big KINDA, my friend."

Kevin looked up at last from his half-eaten meal to look Kyle in the eye. "I really like this girl. She could be the one, Kyle."

Kyle was entering new territory with his friendship with Kevin. Preparing his response carefully he replied, "Let me ask you a very important question; take your time to answer. How strongly do you feel about the job offer in Houston?"

Kevin swallowed his bite of omelet and responded, "It's just a job, Kyle."

Kyle needed more information at this point, "You need to expand on that for me."

Kevin obliged, "Look, the offer is not my first choice. I interviewed with them as a backup for McDaniel Exploration, the place I really want to work."

Kyle's curiosity was now piqued. "Why McDaniel?"

Kevin's response was well rehearsed as if he had shared this story more than once before. "McDaniel is making a difference not just in the way they go about exploration, but their focus on their employees is world class. The founder, Dave McDaniel, is a leader who gets it and is someone I want to learn from."

"What does he get?" asked Kyle. "He gets life is bigger than the bottom line. He gets it is about the people. Get the people part right and the bottom line takes care of itself. Their results speak for themselves. Even as a mid-sized exploration group, I really think there is tremendous potential there."

Kyle had always had a soft spot for someone with this much passion. He looked across the table at Kevin and said, "I am sold. Let's put together a plan to make this happen. I think there is a path to capture the girl's heart and the job you want. You in?"

Kevin's expression must have shown a tiny bit of disbelief given Kyle's follow-up question, "Kevin, you have to be all in if you are in."

Kevin gathered his composure and responded, "I'm all in. Now what?"

Mac had finished his coffee by now. A quick check of the instruments to ensure they were still on course and he offered his thoughts. "The early days were interesting."

"How so?" Kyle asked.

"In the early days the focus on our Kings had a different flavor, Kevin's story is a great example."

"I'm not sure I'm tracking, my friend," Kyle questioned.

Mac didn't miss a beat with his response, "Your early Kings all had one thing in common: purpose. You took Kevin on as a client because he had an 'others first' purpose. He wanted to make a difference in the lives of other people, not just in the bottom line." Mac added, "Look at Kevin now, CEO of McDaniel AND married to Lindsey. With no scandal I might add," Mac continued, "Clara was the same story. She wanted to make a difference in the lives of others and you helped her become U.S. Congresswomen from the Great State of Texas. See the pattern."

Kyle seemed intensely focused on the view in front of him as he processed what Mac was saying. For good measure Mac added, "Kit has fallen for a reason, and my belief is when we get to The Lazy Deuce, we will find a similar situation with Michael."

Kyle asked, "What situation, Mac?"

"The simple fact is Kit and Michael are in for themselves and no one else. Their purpose is self first, others . . . well, others last, to be blunt," Mac said with a slight elevated tone in his voice.

Kyle nodded silently in agreement, checked the GPS, and said, "Well, we will find out if your theory holds water in a few minutes, we are 60 miles out; prepare for landing."

THE LAZY DEUCE

Kyle taxied the Gulfstream into position just off the main runway of the private landing strip on the Lazy Deuce Ranch. The 25,000-acre ranch sat just north and east of Jackson, Wyoming. The ranch had been a 10-year project of Michael's. The main house, which sat five miles off the closest main highway, was called Prima Hora, Latin for "the first hour." It covered 15,000 square feet and was well positioned to capture the sweeping views of the mountain ranges that surrounded the ranch.

Security at the ranch was tight during normal operations, but as Kyle and Mac were being driven to the main house from the airfield, it became apparent that security had been increased to extreme levels. In addition to Michael's normal detail of Navy Seal-trained personal security detail, he had acquired the services of former Secret Service Special Agent, Todd Nelson. Mac had heard of Todd, but their paths had never crossed.

The black Suburban slowed as it approached the first of two checkpoints leading up to the main house. Highly trained dogs quickly circled the vehicle while one individual used a mirror to check the undercarriage of the Suburban. Mac leaned over close to Kyle to speak softly, "This seems a bit tighter than I anticipated." Kyle nodded in agreement.

After another 400 yards they pulled up to the main gate of Prima Hora. Todd Nelson himself greeted Kyle and Mac with an outreached hand as he opened the door on Kyle's side of the truck. "I appreciate your patience with the added measures. Michael and his wife have been rattled and he insisted on tight lockdown," Todd explained as he firmly shook hands with Kyle. Mac had climbed out of his side of the vehicle and made his way to the other side to greet Todd.

"Pleasure to meet you," Mac said with a firm professional tone.

"Likewise. Let's get you two inside to speak with the boss," Todd said as he turned and motioned toward the main doors of the home.

Kyle never noticed, but Mac immediately picked up the two men shadowing them from a distance. Todd's keen sense of observation prompted him to speak, "Guests at the main house have a guardian angel watching over them at all times."

Kyle, not aware of the additional people, asked, "Guardian angel?"

Todd smiled knowing he should have provided more detail. "Yes, both of you will have a personal protection detail assigned to you during your stay on the property. They will always be out of sight, but rest assured they are always close by if needed."

At that moment Kyle could feel his heart race in his chest as the seriousness of the situation began to sink in.

Walking through the massive hand-carved doors, Kyle and Mac found themselves in the center of a round entryway large enough to park several cars. From the semi-round stairway to the left of the entry, Kyle heard the familiar voice of Michael Allen calling his name.

"Kyle, Mac, thank God you're here. This has been one crazy day," Michael offered before reaching the bottom step. "Come into my office so we can talk." Without stopping at the bottom step, Michael grabbed Kyle's hand to both shake and guide him to his office. Kyle needed no help in getting to Michael's office, having spent a considerable amount of time there over the years. Michael's grip on Kyle's hand was much more than a guiding hand, Kyle could sense the comfort Michael received from being close to his friend, The Kingmaker.

The office was designed to hold Michael's extensive book collection numbering well over 5,000 with many being first editions. Positioned in the middle of the sprawling, round-shaped room were two overstuffed, tufted leather sofas accompanied by two smaller versions of the same design in addition to the two high-back armchairs covered in an exotic animal hide. Directly across the room from the double door entry was a towering fireplace with a smooth river stone facade rising to a height of 24 feet in the air. The mountain air had just the right amount of briskness to permit a small fire in the massive hearth. Michael's desk, positioned to one side of the room, was more of a working layout table than a traditional office desk. The 12-foot table was built of reclaimed wood harvested from a 100-year-old barn located on the north side of The Lazy Deuce. Spread across the table were architectural drawings along with a small study model of a mixed-use development plan.

"What will you have to drink?" Michael offered as he made his way to the section of the library containing the multiple shelves of liquor and wine. "I can have a wine brought up from the cellar if you prefer," Michael continued. As Michael poured himself a scotch with ice, Kyle responded, "Diet Coke if you have one." Anticipating the answer, Michael reached into the concealed refrigerator producing Kyle's request. Handing Kyle his drink, Michael spoke in a low, almost whisper tone, "Kyle, I really need your help on this one."

"That's why I'm here, my friend. Why don't you fill me in on how it got to this point."

Michael placed one hand on Kyle's shoulder to move him to the layout table containing the architectural plans. "You are looking at the catalyst for the storm upon us. The development is called

'Prime Harbor,' a mixed-use development on some of the most valuable land in the country."

"I remember the first pitch you made to me on this over two years ago. So, this is it," Kyle remarked. "I don't recall anything in the initial presentation that sounded controversial. How did we get here?"

Michael stepped away from the desk and slowly walked toward the bar to refresh his drink. Without turning around he answered Kyle, "It seems the project has grown out of control, and portions of the land were a bit more difficult to acquire than I originally thought they would be."

"Michael, I've never heard you talk about a difficult deal since I have known you."

Michael looked up from pouring his drink, paused, and with an unrehearsed dramatic tone said, "I have never run up against the Russian mob before today."

Kyle instinctively glanced toward Mac who had slipped into an out-of-the-way position where he could keep a close watch on all parties. Mac's facial expression told Kyle all he needed to know— this was not good. Kyle paused for a moment before responding, "We have to continue to take these threats to your life very seriously. What else do we need to know?"

Michael motioned with his hand for Kyle to sit while he joined him in the center of the room. "It seems these people have deep connections with cyber-terrorists who launched a series of attacks on our main servers. They seem to be targeting our financials and my level-one personal files."

Kyle immediately chimed in, "Has the FBI been brought in yet?"

"Yes, Special Agent Todd has been assigned to look into the matter. What he can't do is manage the PR nightmare that we are facing here. If Prime Networks gets pulled into this ordeal, it would be devastating. My Board will have a heyday with this and certainly will ask for me to tender my resignation."

Kyle pulled out his phone to take a few notes while Michael was talking. Looking up from his phone, he said, "Michael, I understand why they would target your financials, but what do they have to gain from your personal files?"

Michael placed his drink on the side table, leaned forward and spoke in a soft, almost whispered voice. "These files are more than just my personal files. Level-one files have the highest encryption possible and contain insider information. The fact they know of their existence is scary in and of itself."

"What will they find on these files?" Kyle asked.

"Complete details to the Prime Harbor deal along with every other deal I have ever completed," Michael answered. "Look, Kyle, to become a billionaire you are going to have to make some people mad along the way. That's just part of it. These level-one files are a complete listing of all those people with enough information to create a world-class catastrophe for me and Prime Networks."

Kyle was now scrolling through his contact list looking for a name. He spoke to Michael without looking up from his phone, "How good is your head of IT security?" Michael gave Kyle of look of disappointment and replied, "He is the best money can buy."

Kyle's eyes grew closer together and said, "Sometimes it's not about what money can buy, but who is the best. In this case you are going to need a blackhat. It just so happens I know the right person for the job." With that comment he hit send on his phone. Mac nodded as his phone vibrated in his hand, knowing what needed to be done. Silently, he slipped into the main entry to send a text to Susan Hall, a blackhat hacker that Mac had saved from a life behind bars. Within moments Mac had received a text back with a simple three-letter code that only the two of them knew. She was in.

Mac came back into the library, glanced at Kyle, gave a nod indicating Susan was in, and resumed his observation duties. Kyle leaned back into the overstuffed sofa and said to Michael, "Tell your IT department we will take it from here." Michael's look was one of half disgust and half joy, as he knew Kyle would get the job done. Michael's disappointment came from the fact that he had been unable to defeat this enemy on his own.

"Michael, answer a question for me."

"Name it," Michael answered getting up from his seat to pour himself yet another drink.

Kyle spoke softly yet firmly, "You have more money than you could ever need. How did it get to this? This was not the path you told me you wanted to take those many years ago when we first connected."

Michael stopped what he was doing, put down the bottle of scotch and looked at Kyle. "Kyle, I don't know what happened. What I do know is there is never enough." With those words Kyle knew there had been a seismic shift in the thinking of his old friend.

The phone in Mac's pocket vibrated, alerting him to an incoming text message. He glanced at the screen and read the message from Susan, *"Found the hack. Morons used my code to create a backdoor. Door closed! Will monitor as we discussed."*

Mac slipped in behind Kyle and leaned into his ear. "Files are secure. We set up surveillance as planned," Kyle nodded. Mac effortlessly made his way back to his post and surveyed the room one additional time.

Kyle stood up and walked over to the large model on the desk. "We have the hacking under control for now and will monitor the situation going forward."

Michael shook his head in disbelief. "I have had an entire department working on this problem for over a week with no progress and you fix this in less than a hour. I'm going to fire everyone in my IT group."

"Hardly necessary," Kyle responded.

The pieces of the puzzle began to come together for Kyle as they stood in the room. Michael only hires the best talent. So, why the delay in IT when the firm has been under cyber attack? Multiple scenarios began to form in Kyle's mind. First, he began to feel like it was an inside job. Second, the lack of loyalty from Michael's team was coming more into focus. Kyle knew he would find answers to these questions and others once he had a chance to speak to Susan.

It was early in the morning before the men found their way to a bed for a few hours of sleep. Sunrise was on its way and additional planning would need to be discussed over breakfast. Mac was the first up, having slept for only two hours. He made a sweep of the house grounds before coming into the kitchen area to begin preparing breakfast, knowing the staff at the ranch had been reduced to a minimum given the security threat. Around mid-morning, both Michael and Kyle felt confident that the plan they had put together would keep the Board of Directors satisfied – at least for the moment.

Taking the last sip of his coffee Kyle asked Michael the question that had nagged at him all night. "Michael, I know you have enemies outside the firm. How many do you have inside the firm?"

Michael's facial expression stiffened as he answered, "Kyle, don't be naïve, I'm not in a popularity contest. Business is war; even the greatest generals were hated by their troops. Of course, there are people who don't like my tactics or me. That comes with the job."

"How could you let it go this far, Michael? You are at the top."

Michael gave Kyle a very cool stare before responding, "Old friend, don't you know that I learned all I know from the Kingmaker?"

The silence between the two men approached the awkward stage as Kyle processed Michael's remarks. Breaking the silence as she entered the room from the back stairway was Michael's wife, Mackenzie. Her long dark hair was pulled into a ponytail, and she was wearing grey sweatpants and an oversized sweatshirt and dark-rimmed glasses. Even with no makeup, Mackenzie's natural beauty radiated throughout the room. Her unassuming appearance disguised the fact that she was an upcoming power player on Wall Street. With an MBA from Wharton, Mackenzie was a departure from Michael's previous wives as she was every bit his equal in business.

She approached Kyle, kissing him on the cheek. "Thank you for being here."

Kyle could sense the exhaustion in Mackenzie's voice. He reached for a cup to pour her some coffee as he responded, "Anytime Kenz. Em said to tell you 'hi.'" Mackenzie's face showed signs of life at the mention of Emily. "I so miss her. How is she?"

"In desperate need of a girls' weekend. You two need to connect." Mackenzie smiled as she held her coffee close to her face to feel its warmth. "A girls' weekend sounds so delightful right now."

Michael had slipped out of the room to get an update on the day's schedule leaving Kyle and Mackenzie alone in the kitchen. "I overheard the question you asked Michael."

"Which one?" Kyle asked.

Mackenzie took a slow sip of coffee then answered, "The one about enemies. The answer is 'yes.' Michael has made some serious enemies inside the firm. I am starting to see a side of him that I didn't know existed."

"What do you mean?" Kyle asked.

Mackenzie replied, "He's become overly obsessed with building his empire."

Kyle responded quickly, "Michael has always been driven, Kenz."

"Not like this, Kyle. Over the last year he has been putting together deals that don't make financial sense. They seem to be almost vindictive in nature. For all his faults, Kyle, I have always believed Michael to be honest man. But something clearly has changed."

Kyle gave a Mackenzie a kiss on the forehead. "I have to go. We need to continue this conversation when you are back in the City."

Mackenzie smiled and said, "It was great seeing you. Give Em my love."

With that Kyle turned toward the door where Mac was waiting with their bags. "We are wheels up in 30 minutes," Mac announced as Kyle came through the door.

"Great. We have much to talk about on the ride back," Kyle said as the two men climbed into the black SUV.

THE REVELATION

As the wheels of the Gulfstream lifted off the ground, Kyle quickly made the necessary adjustments to navigate their way back to the City. "Should be a smooth flight home; weather is going to cooperate," Mac announced over the headset. Kyle stared ahead out the plane's front window, running the last 48 hours through his brain. Mac was correct; the events of the recent collapse of two of his kings were starting to create a pattern.

His trance was broken as Mac handed him fresh coffee. "This is far better than that brew at the ranch," Mac said as he offered the cup to Kyle.

"Thanks, Mac." Taking a sip, his face revealed the delight of the crisp brew. "Mac, something Mackenzie said before we left has me considering what you said . . . about a pattern developing."

Mac, understanding the teachable moment, responded appropriately, "Tell me more."

Kyle continued, "It seems both Kit and Michael have a common theme in their collapse: greed."

Mac knew to keep his response to questions at this point, "What do you suspect drove that greed?"

Kyle took another long sip of coffee before responding, "I'm not completely sure."

In an effort to help Kyle discover this truth on his own, Mac continued to probe, "Sometimes, if you consider the counterpoint, you can see the point more clearly. Take Kevin, for example. He has continued to remain successful. What is the contrast between the three of them?"

In his head, Kyle began to review systematically Kevin's story before answering Mac. "On the surface it would seem Kevin's motivation was different than Kit's and Michael's."

"How so?" asked Mac.

"Kevin seemed to be focused on others first where Kit and Michael seem to be focused primary on themselves."

Mac wanted to ensure Kyle was tracking fully on this line of thinking, "Business can be brutal, so don't you have to look out for yourself to survive?" he asked.

Kyle reached to make an adjustment to their setting based on updated information from Air Traffic Control as they headed toward the Chicago area. Once the updates between him and the

ATC were completed, his mind reengaged into the conversation. "Yes, Mac, business is brutal. But, it seems there are two schools of thought on how to fight the battle."

Mac began to smile on the inside as he could sense his friend getting closer to the truth. "What are the two thoughts?" Mac asked.

"It seems one school of thought is I can get anything and everything I want by using everyone around me to achieve my success. The other school seems to be that I can achieve all I want if I help others achieve what they want."

Mac grinned with approval of Kyle's insight. "So, working off your premise of two schools of thought, what would you suspect drives an individual one way or the other?" Mac asked.

Kyle struggled a moment as he tried to respond, "Dang it, Mac, I hate it when you do that."

"Do what?" Mac said with the slightest of grins.

"Reach into my head that way," Kyle shot back.

"So, what is inside your head at this moment?" Mac asked.

"The answer is purpose. It's purpose, Mac, and I know that because I had purpose at one point and now see the same thing happening to me as is happening to the others."

Mac knew this was a tender moment for Kyle so he treaded carefully, "What thing is happening, my friend?"

"I feel myself beginning to use others as a means to an end. Beginning with Em. I used to have the sense of a higher calling in creating kings. Now, it feels like it is all about building a bigger kingdom, about playing the chess game, same as Kit and Michael."

Kyle's revelation was more than Mac could have hoped for. His friend was discovering a key principle in life: *a person whose life is purpose-centered, and committed to investing in others, yields a greater return than a life centered on self.*

The flight home seemed to go by in half the time as the two men engaged in their conversation. Kyle taxied the Gulfstream toward the hanger as Mac texted for the car to be brought from the parking garage. With the final post-flight checks completed Mac gathered the bags and headed for the car. Kyle remained in his seat for just a brief moment as he held his phone in his hand. Staring at the screen he tapped on the text message icon and scrolled down to the last conversation he had with Em. Slowly he typed his message to her, *"Just landed. Looking forward to dinner.*

I truly missed you. " With that he climbed out of the captain's seat and departed the plane.

Em was in the park for a late afternoon run when her phone vibrated in her hand. She glanced down to see the notification from Kyle and slowed her pace to read the message. When she opened the full message her already elevated heart rate raced a tad more. With sweat dripping from her nose onto the screen of her phone, she tapped in the following message, *"Glad you are safe. Reservations at 7:00 steak house. I missed you, too."* A slight grin of guarded optimism spread across her face as she continued her run, this time with a noticeably increased pace.

***

From the day it opened with its modern industrial deco and quality meats, the steak house at the corner of 58th and 6th Street had been a regular hangout for Kyle and Emily. The executive chef knew both by name and never missed the opportunity to spend time tableside when they were in the restaurant. Mac dropped them off just before 7:00 and asked when he should be back. "I think we will walk home tonight Mac. Head home. See you in the morning." Mac nodded at Kyle, knowing that tonight was an opportunity to correct some past wrongs between the two of them. "Thanks, boss. Reach out if I can help with anything."

Upon entering the nondescript door Kyle and Emily were guided to their favorite table. Two glasses of their favorite wine sat tableside, ready for pouring. No menus were necessary as their server poured their wine and delivered warm, house-baked bread to the table. Within moments of being seated, the Chef appeared, kissing Emily on both cheeks like a long-lost sister he hadn't seen in months. Following a briefing on the special items he was working on in the kitchen, the two decided on dinner. In an instant they found themselves alone with no one and nothing to distract them. After a momentary pause Kyle picked up his glass to offer a simple toast for the evening. "Moments like this with you are my greatest joy in life." Emily raised her glass and gently touched hers to his, holding hers in place for an extended moment as she made deliberate eye contact with Kyle. She knew from years of experience that something was brewing in his head and that he wasn't just being "on" as Kyle often had to do while playing his "role" in large groups. Kyle's eyes never lied. Emily knew at once Kyle was contemplating something larger than work, which could only mean one thing: his thoughts revolved around the two of them.

After taking a sip of wine, Emily broke the brief silence, "That may be the sweetest thing you have said to me in years. It almost makes me worried there is a 'but' yet to come."

Kyle faked a grin and responded, "No 'buts' tonight, just dinner."

Emily smiled back while taking another sip of wine. Kyle struggled inside to share with Em his revelation and how it has impacted their relationship. For a man known as the Kingmaker, he suddenly found himself paralyzed by fear as he sat across from his greatest personal triumph – and failure. He knew in his heart of hearts that Em was slowly slipping away and still no words formed in his head to save her.

Dinner arrived to the table creating the distraction Kyle needed. The meal was a visual work of art presented with pride by the Chef himself. Emily feasted upon the perfect culinary display, wishing the entire time she had more of an appetite. She could sense Kyle's reluctance to talk about anything other than the most benign subjects. Kyle, as per his usual, found comfort in his food as he slowly but deliberately worked his way through the prime cut of steak before him. After a second bottle of wine and bowl of house-made ice cream, the two came to the end of their meal. As Kyle signed the check, he asked Em if she was still up for a walk home. "I think the walk will do me some good after all the food I just consumed," Emily said.

There were several options for the walk home; tonight Kyle considered the route through the park the best choice. The couple crossed 59th street and entered the park on Center Drive. The City was filled with a symphony of sounds and smells. Even at the late hour the park played host to several thousand people, mostly tourists haggling with local artists selling their works. Kyle and Emily walked for several minutes without speaking – something both had become accustomed to when in each other's presence. Upon reaching the carousel, Emily paused for a moment as she stared fondly at the beautifully painted horses. Having spent time working with the Central Park Conservatory, the carousel held a special place in Emily's heart. Kyle paused with Emily, feeling the urge to check his phone for updates to the crisis of his two fallen kings. Emily turned to Kyle who had wandered a few steps away and broke the silence by asking Kyle a direct question, "Do you still love me, Kyle?"

The matter-of-fact nature in which Emily asked the question caught Kyle off guard. "Of course I do. Why would you ask such a question?" Kyle responded knowing full well why she was asking.

Emily, not moving from her spot, looked Kyle directly in the eyes and answered, "The story I am writing in my head about us has changed from the early days. The story began with purpose and a passion to help others achieve their greatest dream, which included me. That story has changed, Kyle. It is no longer driven by purpose. The story that is being written today is one of only you."

Kyle could feel his heart racing as he searched for the right words. The master of communication suddenly found himself preparing his thoughts as if he was his own client. Before Kyle could speak, Emily continued. "I know what's going on with Michael. Mackenzie called me shortly after you left the ranch. I learned about Kit yesterday. I appreciate you taking time to have dinner with me tonight given all that is happening. I knew there was a but that was coming, I just didn't realize at the moment it was going to come from me."

Kyle's faced showed a confused look as he finally spoke, "What are you saying, Em?"

Emily's eyes became moist as she tried to speak, "I'm saying your greatest joy in life was moments with me, but you have changed the story, Kyle, and moments with me are no longer in the storyline. If the last chapter of this story has us together, we are going to need help getting there."

Kyle stood silently in the glow of the park lights as he processed Emily's words. The severity of what he was hearing began to sink in as he realized he was on the brink of losing the love of his life. Everything Kyle thought to say seemed inadequate at the moment, "I don't want to lose you."

Emily turned toward home and walked slowly along the path. Kyle, never far from her side, walked silently along with her. Within a few minutes they arrived at their building on Central Park West and made their way to their home on the top floor. Kyle felt the weight of Emily's words pressing in on his chest. Needing to catch his breath and collect his thoughts he headed into his office. Kyle's office, which overlooked the park, was a favorite retreat for him to unwind and reflect. Kyle sat motionlessly staring at the glow of the City lights, which filled the windows of the pre-war, penthouse apartment. The minutes turned into hours. About 2:00 in the morning, exhaustion overcame him and he nodded off to sleep.

THE RUN

Kyle rounded the curve on Central Drive where it turned into East Drive and picked up his pace. Between the collapse of his clients and now what appeared to be the collapse of his marriage, Kyle's Sunday morning, head-clearing run would need to be extended. Looking up, Kyle realized he was now passing the carousel in the park – another reminder of the previous evening's conversation with Emily. Once again, his heart rate increased to match yet another pace change. As he continued his run, thoughts of the last several days flooded his mind. Kyle normally found great comfort managing multiple projects and events simultaneously, but today was different. Today he was consumed with thoughts of Emily and all that she had challenged last night. But he also was torn because, to save his clients, his feelings for Emily needed to wait. If he had said it once, it had been said a million times, "The client always comes first." These words had been so engrained into Emily's mind that frequently she would say it before Kyle even had a chance. Little did Kyle realize: Each time Emily said it, a small piece of her and their marriage died.

***

Passing the boathouse on his left, Kyle's continued his quickened pace through the park. The time alone helped him unearth clarity as to what needed to be done to help his clients. First was Kit. From the beginning Kyle knew what he was getting into with a client like this. A hard-charging, do-whatever-it-takes kind of person, Kit was wired for success. And while Kyle was confident he would be able to save Kit this time around, he wondered how many more times like this there might be. And yet, given the fees generated from Kit's company, shouldn't Kyle be grateful for each of Kit's misgivings? Over the years Kyle had learned to justify the less-than-desirable behavior that seemed to be a DNA trait of successful, driven leaders. But then there was Kevin. Because of him, Kyle knew it actually was possible to be a king and leave a positive mark on the world; it all depended on the king's purpose.

The Park was beginning to show signs of life by the time Kyle made his way north along East Drive passing the Met on is right. Kyle couldn't help but think back to a time when Emily, Michael, and Mackenzie enjoyed one of the hidden treasures in the City: lunch on the rooftop of the Met. Very few even knew there was a rooftop let alone a small bistro and spectacular panoramic views of the City. As Kyle continued to replay that autumn afternoon memory, he was reminded of a side conversation he and Michael shared while standing along the edge of the roof, eating a gourmet turkey sandwich. The details of the conversation seemed less important than the statement Michael made at the end. As the girls were wrapping up their chat, Michael, with a glass of wine in one hand, put his other arm around Kyle and in a voice shared in a hushed tone, leaned forward into the group and proclaimed, "I have learned more from this man than anyone in my life. THREE CHEERS TO THE KINGMAKER."

As Kyle's heart raced, his body temperature soared. The memory of that rooftop moment immediately reminded him of Michael's last words at the ranch, "I've learned from the best." A wash of anxiety came over Kyle as he considered the impact he had had on his kings and the predicaments they now found themselves in. Was it possible that he had been part of the problem? As the ramifications of this question ran a loop in Kyle's mind, a strong wave of nausea overtook him. Kyle pulled up from his 8-minute-mile pace and veered to the far side of the trail. Trees lined the path along East Drive, affording Kyle just the leaning post he needed as the contents of his insides made themselves known. With little in his stomach, his vomiting quickly advanced to dry heaves. The increased pain in his abdomen quickly moved into his chest. Within moments he found himself on his knees in pain, tears streaming down his face and torrents of sweat pouring from his brow. His right arm began to throb. He was flush, lightheaded and desperately trying to catch his breath. But then all went dark.

Kyle squinted as he focused his eyes on the letters before him. FDNY came into clear view as the paramedic listened to Kyle's heart through her stethoscope. But the fogginess in his head seemed intent to hang on longer than the blurriness of his vision. Even the slightest head movement proved painful, especially once he noticed a second gloved paramedic holding a strip of blood-soaked gauze. A small early morning crowd had gathered to do what New Yorkers do: *watch*.

"Sweetie," the young female paramedic said softly to Kyle, "we are going to take you to Mount Sinai for a few stitches and have you checked out. Do you remember what happened?"

Trying to gather his thoughts Kyle instinctively reached for his phone. Looking up at the paramedic he did his best to form words, but nothing came. Kyle simply stared with a look of hopelessness at those treating him, indicating he didn't remember what happened. "Don't you worry, sweetie, we are only a few minutes away. You are going to be just fine. Is there someone you want to call?" Still not able to speak, Kyle nodded, tapped his phone and gingerly handed it to the paramedic. Seeing the phone was dialing, she took the phone from Kyle, tapped the speaker button, and waited for an answer.

"Morning, boss," came the voice over the speaker.

"Mac," Kyle said with a shaky, unrecognizable voice. Interceding on Kyle's behalf the young paramedic spoke up, "Hi, Mac? This is Clara Parker with the NYFD. Your friend has taken a spill of sorts in the Park. We are on our way to Mount Sinai if you would like to meet him there."

Mac was already en route to the car after hearing Kyle's voice. "Thanks, Clara. I will be there in 10 minutes. His name is Kyle Ellis in case he didn't have his ID with him this morning."

Clara smiled as she listened to Mac and looked at Kyle, "Well hello there, Mr. Ellis. You are going to be just fine. Let's get you going." Moments later Kyle was loaded and en route to Mount Sinai.

The ride was only a few blocks and by the time they arrived to the hospital, Kyle's voice had returned with noticeable strength. "Thank you, Clara," were Kyle's first substantial words. Clara was looking over the EKG tape that had been running when Kyle spoke. She smiled as she turned toward him and said, "No thanks needed; that's my job. Can you remember what happened now?" she continued.

Kyle closed his eyes as to recall a dream and softly said, "I remember feeling dizzy and then getting sick as I leaned against a tree. But then, nothing."

The large red and white truck pulled into the Emergency drive, quickly unloaded Kyle en route to the ER. Clara and her partner began downloading information to the tending physician as they continued to roll Kyle down the hallway. Within moments a symphony of nurses, guided by a single doctor, were reviewing Kyle's case.

Clara squeezed her way bedside to take Kyle's hand one last time. "You are in the best hands now, Sweetie." And with that she disappeared behind the blue drape that divided the rooms.

Mac made his way into the ER to locate Kyle's room. The Chief of Plastic Surgery was just readying himself to give Kyle the first of 10 stitches needed on the right side of his head just behind the ear. A perfectly timed phone call from Mac while en route to the hospital ensured the top people in the hospital were available in the ER that Sunday morning. Kyle saw Mac from a few feet away and smiled at the sight of his old friend.

"Looks like you got mugged," Mac said with a bit of humor in his voice.

"Nothing so exciting I'm afraid, Mac. Seems I passed out and hit my head," Kyle explained with the full strength of his voice. "While you were running?" Mac asked with a concerned look on his face. "Worse," said Kyle. "I had stopped to throw up and that's what did it."

To the right of the bed stood Dr. Leslie Katz, the on-call cardiologist reading a long folded strip of paper. "It would appear that the event was brought on by either a mild heart attack or an extreme anxiety attack. We will know more after a few tests."

Both Mac and Kyle looked at each other with a concern and confusion. "Did you call Em?" Kyle asked. "Sent her a text; she is at church this morning," Mac responded.

Kyle closed his eyes knowing that he should have been there with her. Dr. Katz put his hands on the side of the bed railing and leaned over Kyle slightly. "We are going to prepare a room for you to keep you for further observation." With those words Mac stepped aside and began updating Emily. Kyle motioned for Mac. "Mac, do you believe in premonitions?"

"How do you mean?" Mac asked.

"The last several hours I have had this feeling the world is trying to tell me something," Kyle said. The team of doctors and nurses looking on all smiled in concert at hearing Kyle's remarks.

Mac grinned and replied, "Well, you did just have a serious event take place, and there is that nasty blow to the head."

Kyle cut Mac off before he could finish, "I need you to do something for me."

"Name it, boss."

"Reach out to Clara Becker and set up a time to meet. I will go to her if necessary. Also, send flowers to Clara Parker with a note saying, '*Thank you for being my angel in more ways than one.*' Seems young Ms. Clara has been inadvertently telling me something. I need to speak with the Congresswomen, face to face."

Mac nodded his head as he was making notes in his phone and then responded, "Heard."

***

Emily appeared inside the draped-off space and found Kyle resting. She stood quietly looking down at the man she loved still wearing his running shorts and now-stained-with-blood shirt. The monitors next to Kyle's bed told a story of peaceful rest, which was more than could be said for Emily at that moment. She gently reached and took ahold of his hand as Kyle's eyes fluttered open. In a groggy voice Kyle said, "So sorry about this. So sorry about everything."

Emily smiled and squeezed Kyle's hand even more firmly. "You've created quite the commotion," she said to lighten the moment. She knew his apology came from the drugs but still held to the eternal hope that deep inside he really felt that way. A brief instant later, Kyle drifted back off to sleep leaving Emily alone to wonder.

THE CONGRESSWOMAN

Kyle would not be cleared to fly for another two weeks, so Mac sat in the captain's seat on their way to Kyle's ranch in Texas. Kyle had convinced his doctors that he and Em would follow doctor's orders carefully to ensure a quick recovery from what turned out to be a mild heart attack. The trip actually had a hidden agenda that only Kyle and Mac knew. Congresswoman Clara Becker was going to be spending time in her home district in Texas and changed her schedule to meet with Kyle at Warwick Ranch just outside of Junction, Texas. Mac coordinated the flight plan to land in Austin to pick up the Congresswoman so that the group could fly to Warwick together. When Emily noticed the plane descending Kyle came clean on the agenda for the weekend. "So much for following your doctor orders of NO work this weekend," Em said in a scolding tone.

Kyle looked at Emily with an apologetic look and explained, "No work, Em. Just two old friends catching up. That's all." Em knew better and communicated as much through the look she gave Kyle in return.

"Great. I haven't seen Clara since last Christmas. It will be good to catch up," Em said making it clear that she knew what was going on.

Mac guided the Gulfstream into the private hanger to meet Clara and her staff. Her team of eight was dutifully standing by to handle any needs the Congresswoman had. Much of her team had been with her from the beginning of her tenure in D.C. As a six-term U.S. Representative and from the state of Texas, Clara was among the highest ranking members in the House. On the Hill, she was known as the straight shooter from Texas because of her unique ability to operate with true integrity within a city that found an ever-shifting integrity to be the norm.

Standing just over 5' 8", Clara was an athletic, attractive woman who presented herself with a disarming charm. Her smile would neutralize even the toughest opponent in any debate. Kyle and Clara first met while attending the University of Texas. Both were scholarship athletes in somewhat similar sports. Kyle played baseball, Clara softball. But it wasn't sports that connected their paths. Clara caught Kyle's attention when she decided to run for student body president her junior year in school. Kyle and Emily had only been on a few dates when the school elections began. It was during one of those few dates Kyle asked Emily to attend an early debate between Clara and her male challenger. Not a girl's dream date, but Emily agreed, as she was certainly intrigued with getting to know Kyle Ellis more. During the debate Clara's challenger made the decision to attack the fact Clara was a female and simply not qualified to be student body president. It was Clara's response that instantly made the connection for Kyle. Clara chose, at that debate, to take the high road and not join into the gender debate trap that was being set by her opponent. In return, Clara did something so surprising Kyle remembered it for years: Clara praised her opponent, speaking to his unique qualifications to be the school president. While the tactic was daring, it proved unsuccessful. Even still, Kyle had to meet this person. And once he did, the seeds to Kyle's future career as the Kingmaker were planted.

As Mac descended the stairs of the Gulfstream to greet the Congresswoman, Kyle could hear Clara as she approached the plane. "Sweetie, it's so great seeing you again. It has been too long." Sitting inside the plane a smile came across Kyle's face as he knew at that moment he was where he needed to be.

THE WARWICK RANCH

After the short flight from Austin to the ranch, Mac positioned the plane in the ranch's private hanger. The F350 Super Duty Ford truck made its way up the semi-paved tree-lined road from the landing strip about a mile to the main house on the property. It was about 200 yards from the circle drive until they passed through the large stone entrance to the main house. Above them the words Warwick Ranch soared high above head. The ranch was named for Richard Neville, the 16th Earl of Warwick, also known as the first Kingmaker and served as a constant reminder to Kyle of the danger that comes with the power of being a kingmaker.

By Texas standards the Warwick was a small ranch with only 2,000 acres. The main house was cozy thanks to Emily. As an accomplished interior designer in New York, it was a refreshing treat to unleash her talents on the hill country home referred to simply as *The Hangout.* With soaring open-beam ceilings the main room of the home was filled with natural light from a series of windows lining the top edge of the ceiling. The open concept kitchen with a 12-foot-long eating bar was a main feature of the space. The kitchen flowed seamlessly into the main living space creating a gathering hub. A stained concrete floor flowed into the central visual point of the room, the fireplace. Reaching 30 feet into the air the fireplace was almost large enough for a person to stand upright in the double-sided hearth. The large stone façade was native to the ranch with a 10-foot mantle hewed from a 100-year-old oak tree that had been struck by lightning. You could still see where the massive bolt of lightning impacted the tree.

The furnishings were comfortable and inviting, thus the nickname *The Hangout*. Once people made it into the main room, they seemed to want to stay. When weather permitted Emily had designed either side of the fireplace with floor-to-ceiling 12-foot folding doors that had the ability to transform the main living space into an indoor-outdoor oasis.

Once Clara walked into the main room she proclaimed, "Emily I had forgotten how marvelous The Hangout was. I may never leave." Emily's friend of many years knew exactly what to say to bring encouragement to her heart.

Emily gave Clara a hug and whispered back, "You can stay as long as you wish, my friend, as long as you wish." With that Emily headed for the kitchen to inventory the contents of the pantry for the evening's dinner.

"What can I get you to drink, Clara?" asked Kyle as he walked into the main room.

"Nonsense," replied Clara. "You need to sit down and rest. I can get my own drink and yours. What will you have?"

Standing in amazement, Kyle paused and turned toward Clara. Friendship aside, here was a senior member of the U.S. House of Representatives offering to get him a drink. With a humble smile, Kyle responded, "Thank you, Clara. I will have whatever you have."

Mac had disappeared to gather firewood from the outside woodshed for the evening's fire. Returning to the main house he found Kyle and Clara sitting on the outside deck overlooking the hill country below. The main house was positioned on the highest point within the property, affording it views that completely filled the visual senses.

After dropping the wood to the side of the fireplace, Mac heard Kyle from behind. "Mac, I was replaying the conversation you and I had flying out to see Michael." Kyle continued, "I told her she is either the exception or the rule when it comes to my clients and that is why I needed to see her."

Mac smiled as if he knew the answer but was keeping to himself. Clara, picking up on Mac's subtle expression, asked Mac to grab something to drink and join them. "I would love to but may need to make a run into town for supplies depending on what Emily needs for dinner." With that Mac turned and disappeared into the main house.

"So, Kyle, why do you think I would be the exception within your clients? Is it because you haven't had to keep me from the front page of the *Journal*?"

Kyle smiled at his long-time friend, "That is how I make money, Clara."

"Based on my sources, you have been extra busy with a few kings," Clara offered as she took a sip of her drink.

Kyle, not surprised at her insider knowledge of the events of the last several weeks, responded, "That is exactly my point. Why is there such a predictable pattern with some and less predictable with others?"

"What are you considering predictable, the fact they fell or the fact that others do not?" Clara asked before continuing, "It seems that you expect all to fail in some monumental fashion. It's not a matter of *if* but *when*. Kyle, I will be the first to tell you no one is perfect and we all fall short of the mark from time to time. However, the epic collapses that you are seeing are not normal. There is something bigger happening here. Or should I say, there is something big 'missing' here."

Kyle was intrigued by his friend's thinking and asked for clarity.

"Sweetie, the first thing missing is integrity. Trust me when I tell you I can spot situational integrity from a mile away."

Kyle stopped mid-drink and asked, "Situational integrity? That's a new one for me."

Clara smiled and responded, "It's my own term. It's simple; if integrity is about being honest and having a strong moral core then situational integrity is when you display just enough honesty and moral grounding to get what you want at that moment. Once the moment is passed and you have what you want, then your integrity morphs into something else, normally back to its default state." Clara continued, "In D.C. it has become so common I believe people have accepted situational integrity as the norm."

Kyle caught himself nodding in agreement as his friend spoke. His mind wandering, Kyle could easily connect the idea of situational integrity to the experiences Kit and Michael had created. Blinking himself back into the conversation, Kyle asked, "What is the second thing?"

Clara smiled in her patented disarming way and answered, "The second component is closely connected to the first. I would go as far to say it impacts situational integrity the most."

Kyle's curiosity had piqued. "What is it?" "Purpose." Clara answered in a very matter-of-fact tone of voice.

"Mac said the same thing to me a few days ago," Kyle confessed to his longtime friend. "So I get it; I just don't fully understand it," Kyle continued.

"That is normal. There is a difference between knowing and understanding. I think you taught me that years ago."

Kyle smiled humbly and in a soft voice said, "I seemed to have lost my way on more than one thing from years ago."

The tone of Clara's voice became much more stern as she replied, "As your friend I owe you this feedback. Kyle, you have changed and not for the better. It seems you have lost your purpose center."

Kyle's eyes were moist from hearing the harsh words from his dear friend. Softly he responded, "Mac uses this phrase often, but I guess I hadn't grasped its true meaning before."

The fire in the massive hearth was beginning to crackle as the flames from the mesquite wood began to grow larger. The day was cooling as a light breeze began to gently blow from the north. Clara finished her drink and placed the glass on the side table. Looking at Kyle with great empathy she said, "We are all wired for a purpose. Our purpose is why we are here. Being purpose-centered is when our giftedness is aligned with why we are here. When we are purpose-centered our lives have greater meaning and we begin to thrive in multiple areas of our life. So the reverse is also true. When our daily actions are not consistent with our purpose, the outcome is often situational integrity...or worse." Kyle nodded more noticeably the more Clara spoke. She continued saying, "When we first met back in college, I was so impressed with your passion to help me. Your passion for helping me achieve my highest potential was your purpose, and you are gifted in a very special way to make that happen. That, my dear friend, is what made you the kingmaker. When you drifted away from your purpose center, you began to drift toward situational integrity. "

The knot in Kyle's throat was growing larger as the tears streamed down his cheeks. He lowered his head and began to rub the tears from his eyes as Clara placed her hand upon his shoulder to comfort her dear friend. "Sweetie, I owe much of my success to you and for that I am forever grateful. I appreciate you so much that I owe you this truth."

The wash of emotions flooding over Kyle at that moment was tremendous. He stood up and walked to the edge of the deck and grabbed the pipe railing that encircled the large outdoor space. As he gripped the banister, he closed his eyes and breathed deeply in through his nose. The crisp cool air provided the hoped-for calming effect as he stood silently trying to collect his thoughts. Opening his eyes he stared out over the vast Texas hill country, looking into a burnt orange sky, made beautiful by the setting sun. With his eyes fixed on one spot, he focused his mind on all Clara had shared. He knew what she said was true. He had moved away from his purpose of serving others as they worked to unlock their true potential. Life had become increasingly more about the challenge—a chess game. Through his actions he had been teaching his clients how to play the game as well. By moving away from his purpose center, he also had moved away from Emily. The story had changed; Em was right.

The large doors on either side of the fireplace had been opened to let the cool air refresh the home. Standing just inside the open doors protected from direct sight by the fireplace stood Emily holding two glasses of wine she had poured for Clara and Kyle. Before she could deliver them, she overheard Clara speaking to Kyle. Not wanting to interrupt their conversation, she stood silently just out of sight but still within hearing distance. As Emily listened to their dear family friend share her insights with Kyle, tears began to run down her own cheeks, too. Emily felt a tremendous compassion for the man she loved. She knew he would have a tough road as he struggled to process all he had just heard.

Wiping her cheeks with the back of her hand, she took a deep breath to regain her composure and stepped into the patio. "I thought a nice glass of Hill Country Pinot Noir would hit the spot on this beautiful evening," Emily declared as she walked up to Clara who was still sitting down. As Emily leaned over to offer the glass of wine to Clara, their eyes connected for a brief moment communicating all that needed to be said. Kyle turned from his position at the railing, his eyes still puffy, and walked toward Emily. Extending the glass of wine Emily smiled at Kyle in a way ensuring him of her undying love and commitment. Kyle reached out to take the glass from Emily and squeezed her fingers ever so gently in an effort to acknowledge his love for her.

On cue Mac appeared holding two additional glasses of wine, handing one to Emily and keeping one for himself. Clara stood lifting her glass slightly into the Texas night air and proclaimed a toast: "To great friends who bring out the best in each other because we want the best for each other." And with that all four touched their glasses ever so gently together and simultaneously proclaimed, "Cheers!"

THE TRAIL

Morning came with the euphoric smells of fresh-brewed coffee and bacon. The sun was just cracking the horizon when Mac began cracking eggs. Kyle opened his eyes and realized he had slept beyond 4:30 a.m. for the first time in recent memory. Lying motionlessly in bed Kyle stared into empty space taking in the feeling of complete relaxation. Emily had her head resting on Kyle's shoulder, her hair covering her face exposing only the tip of her nose. That moment Kyle felt a peace he had not felt in several years. Slowly he began to process all that was happening and knew what he needed to do. It was time to get back on track, to re-center his life and return to the purpose that made him the Kingmaker.

Leaning over, Kyle gently kissed Emily on the forehead and slipped out of bed. He slid into his slippers, grabbed his robe and headed toward the magical smells coming from the kitchen. At the edge of the massive kitchen island, Kyle discovered Mac making from scratch his famous down-home biscuits.

Sitting at the far end of the island was Clara, who already was well involved in her eggs, bacon, and coffee. Looking up over her coffee cup, she proclaimed with a hearty bounce in her voice, "Good morning, sunshine."

Kyle's smile was relaxed and genuine as he replied to his dear friend, "Good morning to you, Congresswomen Becker." Kyle knew the formal address always made Clara blush and this morning was no different.

She smiled back at her friend and restarted her assault on Mac's famous scrambled eggs. "Mac, why are your eggs so much better than my eggs?" she asked between bites. Mac grinned and said, "The secret is in the milk and the wrist." Clara stopped mid-bite to look at Mac with a confused expression.

Kyle grinned and offered some clarity. "Mac has been perfecting his fluffy eggs since grad school. He swears it's all in the wrist."

Again, Clara just stared with hopeless confusion at both of them. Mac offered to demonstrate. Taking a small bowl and cracking a few eggs into it, he added a small amount of milk and then began to whisk the eggs with a fork. With the fury of a power tool, Mac whipped the eggs so fast that they began to froth. His performance seemed to stop as quickly as it began, and in one effortless motion, Mac poured the whipped eggs into the cast iron pan. Once the eggs were settled in the hot pan, he began to whip them more, not stopping until they were done. Lifting the pan from the flame he poured the finished product onto a waiting plate.

"Perfection!" Kyle exclaimed as he looked at Mac who turned to Clara and said with a wry smile, "See, all in the wrist." Laughter simultaneously erupted between all three as Emily appeared in the doorway.

"What could be so funny at this hour?" Emily asked as she walked up to Kyle to give him a kiss on the cheek. Kyle, holding a plate with fresh eggs in his hands scooped up a bite and offered it to Emily. "Mac's famous eggs; he says it is all in the wrist." She grinned, took the bite from Kyle, and nodded in joyous agreement. Laughter again filled the room.

Finishing breakfast Kyle stood to begin clearing the plates. "I am thinking about saddling the horses and going for a ride this morning while it's still cool. Anyone interested?" Kyle offered.

Mac was quick to respond, "Not a bad idea. We should check the fence on the north ridge. The ranch foreman thought maybe some of the cattle had slipped over to our neighbor's place."

Clara exclaimed, "Lord knows I love spending time on horseback, but this sounds like an opportunity for Em and me to have the Hangout all to ourselves." Emily nodded in agreement while flashing a grateful smile.

Kyle and Mac walked the 100 yards to the barn in the gray, early-morning light. The eight-stall barn was a Norman Rockwall classic design. Inside two of Kyle's favorite horses stood ready to saddle. Mac stopped at the tack room to gather the tack necessary while Kyle pulled the two horses out from their stalls. Once mounted the two headed north to inspect the fence.

For the first half mile the two rode in silence taking in all the beauty the hill country had to offer. The only sound shared between the two men was the sound of the well-oiled leather saddles as the two made their way along the trail. "Mac, I had forgotten how peaceful life can be."

Mac stood up slightly in his stirrups to look over an upcoming ridge and said, "Some people go their entire life without finding peace." A classic Mac response intended to challenge Kyle's thinking.

"What do you mean? How is that even possible?" Kyle questioned.

"Easy, no purpose center," Mac said as he settled back into his saddle.

Guiding the horses off the main trail they made their way to the fence line on the north end of the property. The ride would increase in complexity for the next two miles as they surveyed the fence for breaks. Mac led the way as the two rode single file for a few hundred feet as the terrain descended at a downward slope. Once the men were able to join up side-by-side, Kyle picked up where Mac had left off. "How is it possible for a person to not have purpose?" Kyle began.

"It isn't that they don't have purpose; we all have a purpose in life. It is simply that they don't know or understand what their purpose center is," Mac explained. Kyle became silent as he processed Mac's last statement. "You are fortunate that you know and understand your purpose center and from that have experienced a peace that most would consider joy," Mac continued.

"Look how easy it was to become off-center," Kyle exclaimed.

"That is one of the real tests of life. Staying calibrated to your purpose center," Mac said. At that moment Kyle pulled his horse to a completed stop. Mac, noticing Kyle had suddenly stopped, pulled his horse around to check on Kyle. "Everything okay?" Mac asked.

"No, it isn't. I owe you an apology, my friend," Kyle exclaimed. "It seems you have been telling me this for a very long time and I have chosen to ignore you. Deliberately, I am ashamed to say. Please forgive me, Mac." No words were exchanged for the next several seconds as the two just sat there quietly on their horses.

Finally, Mac spoke, "You're forgiven, my friend." With that, Kyle smiled and nudged his horse back down the trail.

"There is still work to be done," Mac said as they continued to ride.

"Yes, I know," Kyle answered. "First things first. I have to change my story with Emily," Kyle added. "Here I am one of the most powerful storytellers in the world and I am struggling to change my own story," Kyle said with a sarcastic tone.

"That is not uncommon," Mac offered as comfort. "If you were a client, what would you do?"

Kyle considered the question before he responded. "Two things: First, I would identify the correct story and paint the picture so others would know what to look for."

Mac nodded then said, "Okay, what's next?"

"Second, I would check for blind spots to ensure the true story maintains momentum," Kyle added.

Mac smiled as he witnessed his old friend finding his groove once again. "So, what is the correct story for Em?" Mac asked.

Kyle stopped and rested back into saddle. "The correct story Mac is Emily is my wife, I love her dearly, and my desire is to honor and serve her as she deserves."

Mac slowed his horse, stood in his stirrups, turned and looked at Kyle. "So what does THAT picture look like?"

Kyle gently booted his horse forward and responded to Mac, "It looks like me placing her needs before mine. It looks like the priorities of my day aligning with the priorities of what I say is important to me, mainly Emily."

Topping the farthest ridge north on the property the two came across a break in the barbed-wired fence. Three strands had snapped from the weight of a fallen limb. The wire break created an easy path for the cattle to exit the property. Reaching into his saddlebag Mac produced the tools necessary to make the repair. Kyle removed the limb with the use of a rope and his horse, while Mac made the needed splice. Upon completing the task Kyle reached into his insulated saddlebag and pulled out two cold drinks and bag of beef jerky. Mac's face lit up like a kid on Christmas morning at the site of the homemade jerky and drinks. The two found resting spots under the massive oak that was referred to as North Oak, given that it marked the farthest north boundary of the ranch.

Mac sipped the cold drink and between bites of jerky asked Kyle to continue. "Blind spots?"

Kyle knew what Mac was asking, "Finding the blind spots is sometimes the toughest task. Once you find them, putting guard-rails in place is crucial."

"So what would you consider a blind spot for you?" Mac asked.

"I have three. First, I tuned you out, creating a mentoring void. Second, I canceled my key King debriefs, which were important to hearing two-way feedback. And third, I am missing the spiritual grounding Em and I had when we were first married."

Mac finished off the last of his jerky and stood to brush off his jeans. "This sounds like the beginning of a solid plan." Reaching out his hand, Mac grabbed on and lifted him from his seated position.

"Now I just need to execute," Kyle said walking to his horse.

Mac stepped up into his saddle swinging his leg over the back of his horse. Looking over to Kyle he said, "Executing your plan is much like this trail. There was a clear beginning and a defined end with several challenging periods along the journey. The key to this trail was to keep going, overcoming the obstacles and never going it alone."

Kyle gave a nod of acknowledgment, realizing once again just how fortunate he was to have Mac in his life.

THE CITY

Traffic in Mid-Town was extraordinarily light for a Friday morning. Mac guided the sedan through the many Yellow Cabs that filled the City streets regardless of time of day. Kyle was finishing up a text to Emily in the back seat before they arrived at the One World Trade Center for a visit with Kit.

Kyle: *"Looking forward to dinner tomorrow night. You pick."*

Emily: *"Per Se on Columbus Circle."*

Kyle: *"Perfect! 7:30?"*

Emily: *"Yes. Love you."*

Kyle: *"Love you, too."*

Kyle looked up from his phone as Mac was pulling into the parking garage. Gathering his well-worn leather briefcase, a gift from Emily for their one-year anniversary, Kyle exited the Mercedes and headed to the elevator. "Mac, can you make a 7:30 reservation for me and Em at Per Se on Columbus?"

"Consider it done."

The two entered the elevator and rode in silence for the 50-second ride to Kit's office. Once they exited into the private lobby, Mac departed to the right as Kyle headed into the secured entrance of Kit's office. Today was a debrief on the events of the last several weeks. Kyle's team had managed to keep Kit's exposure to a minimum, spinning the press he did receive in a positive way. No small feat considering the early-on backlash.

Entering the office Kyle found Kit engaged in his daily routine of emails. Looking up from his laptop, Kit's face lit up as soon as he noticed Kyle. "Good Morning!" Kit exclaimed.

"Morning," Kyle said as he headed for the coffee bar in Kit's office.

"Need a refill?" Kyle asked. Kit made his way from behind his desk to meet Kyle in the middle of the office, holding his coffee cup from earlier in the day.

"I am good for now, thanks for asking," Kit replied. Kyle poured himself a cup and turned to face his old friend.

"We seemed to have dodged a bullet on this one," Kyle said as he sipped his coffee. Kit showed the slightest of grins upon hearing these words from Kyle. He knew the work Kyle did behind the scenes to bury the *WSJ* story and keep the SEC to a mere hand slap was nothing short of a miracle. But miracles had become standard fare for the Kingmaker. Through this entire ordeal there was one item that Kyle was not able to fix – Kit's relationship with Howard. To save Kit there were some hard choices that needed to be made, the worst of which assured the loss of Kit's friendship with Howard. To save the friendship Kit needed to come clean and face his accusers. But Kit's unwillingness to admit any wrong meant that there was nothing that Kyle could do to save the friendship.

Without saying a word Kit moved toward the windows to gaze upon the glittering City. "We saw the ugly side of business on this one," Kit proclaimed, never turning from the window. "I know there were some things said along the way and sacrifices made to reach this outcome. Thank you, Kyle, for all you have done."

Kyle knew Kit's moment of sincerity would be short-lived. Walking up next to Kit at the window, Kyle stood looking out to the City. "The day this ordeal began, you, from this very spot, remarked that the Empire State Building had seen a lot but remained sturdy, that it clearly had been built on a solid foundation." Kit nodded his head remembering the moment. Kyle continued, "I made a comment then about being able to stand the test of time when you are built on a solid foundation."

Kit's eyes narrowed as he turned from the window to face Kyle who was still looking at the City below. "Yes, I remember," Kit said with a hint of confusion in his voice.

Kyle turned from the window and came face to face with Kit. "I am worried about your foundation, old friend. I am not sure you will survive another event like this last one," Kyle said in a soft tone.

"I've survived plenty to suggest I will survive plenty more," Kit replied, his voice slightly elevated.

Kyle smiled and replied, "You may be right. There are a number of crisis management shops standing in line to get your business." The direction of the conversation was beginning to frustrate Kit.

"What are you trying to say, Kyle?" Kyle turned back to the window and fixed his eyes upon the majestic sight that was the Empire State building. "Kit, when we first met I was intrigued by your drive and passion for business. But I made one significant error in taking you on as a future king."

"What might that be?" Kit asked.

Kyle, still fixed on the Empire responded, "I failed to check the foundation upon which your kingdom would be built. The assumption I made was that our purposes were aligned. In the process I have let you down."

Kit stood completely still as he processed Kyle's remarks. After a moment of silence, Kit responded, "I am not sure I understand. Today I am the most powerful king on Wall Street. How exactly is that letting me down? I would say I am very successful and in the process you were quite successful also."

Kyle turned toward Kit to respond, "Our definitions of success don't match. I let you down because I failed to ensure your foundation remained solid. To make matters worse, I have strayed from my own definition and in the process have become an enabler to you and your behavior."

Kit paced the floors in the middle of the expansive office, stunned at what he was hearing from Kyle. The most powerful man on Wall Street was, for the first time, at a loss for words. Walking to the coffee bar, he opened the side cabinet door revealing the contents of the office bar. Pulling down a glass Kit poured three fingers of 40-year-old Macallan scotch and in one continuous motion finished the glass only to pour another. Standing facing the bar, holding the freshly poured glass of scotch, Kit finally spoke, "You know, at $10,000 a bottle that's pretty good scotch. Kyle, how many people on this island do you think are having a $10,000 bottle of scotch for breakfast? Wait, I can tell you . . . NONE!" The volume of Kit's voice increased as he spoke. "I'm not sure what definition of success you are using, but this looks like success to me, *old friend*. Just look around you. The art hanging on the walls of this office alone is worth a small fortune. My kingdom is second to none in size and power. How can this NOT be success?" To make his point more dramatic Kit slammed back the glass of scotch and banged the glass onto the granite bar top.

Kyle hung his head quietly as he listened to Kit's response. It had been only a matter of time before this side of Kit would come spilling out. It was the darker side that Kit had learned to manage and keep in the background, a skill he had learned from Kyle. But the mask had come off and the real Kit Jackson was making an appearance. Kyle watched as Kit poured two more glasses of scotch and consumed each one in a single sip. Kyle knew he only had a few precious moments before Kit would forget all that was said and happened. Pulling out his phone, Kyle sent Mac a quick text.

Kyle: *"Kit is drinking, let his EA know. Have car ready in 10."*

Mac: *"Done. Signal if you need help."*

Kyle walked over to Kit who was still standing next to the bar, one hand firmly gripping the neck of the scotch, the other holding the empty glass. The alcohol was beginning to show its effects.

"Why don't you hand me the bottle, Kit?" Kyle said in an even tone. "Mac is bringing the car around. I will take you home."

Kit's voice rose to a new level, "I don't need to go home!"

After years of working with Kit in stressful situations, Kyle knew that Kit was entering a dangerous place. With his most stern voice, a tone of which Kit had only heard a few select times, Kyle made his demand clear, "Kit, you are leaving, NOW!" With a deep sigh, Kit sat the bottle and glass on the bar and walked to get his suit jacket hanging in the closet. Kyle texted Mac as Kit slowly put on his jacket, each of his movements much more deliberate now.

Kyle: *"Heading down now."*

Mac: *"Here."*

Kyle took Kit by the arm and escorted him out the private door to the elevators in the secure area of the offices. Once to the garage Mac stood waiting to help Kyle get Kit into the car. After a few moments they were on their way to Kit's Upper East Side apartment. Pulling out of the garage and making their way over to Church Street, Mac gracefully navigated the downtown streets of the City. In the back seat of the sedan, Kit sat semi-slumped with his head leaning against the door window.

Breaking the silence of the ride, Kit spoke the first words, "You never answered me."

"What is it you want to know?" Kyle replied.

"What is your new, self-righteous definition of success?"

Kyle showed signs of a slight grin as he responded, "Not that you will remember any of this but success is when your purpose, talents, and resources come together to meet the needs of others."

Kit pressed his head even more into the window, his eyes rolling to the back of his head for dramatic effect. Managing to still respond, Kit said, "My companies meet plenty of needs."

Kyle smiled understanding it would take Kit a bit more time to process all that he had heard.

Pulling into the front of Kit's building, his doorman met the car as Mac pulled to a stop. Known for their discretion, the doorman quickly escorted Kit to the private penthouse elevator. Within a matter of moments, Kit was safe in his apartment preparing to sleep off the effects of $10,000 scotch.

* * *

The morning sun produced a crease of light in the master suite of Kit's penthouse apartment. The smell of fresh-brewed coffee filled the air of the expansive room. Kit's head pounded from the hangover that hit him full force. Cracking his eyes open just wide enough to see the time on the bedside clock, Kit discovered on his nightstand the steaming cup of coffee, bottled water, and two tablets for his headache. Knowing Sara was at their Hampton's house with the staff, the cup of coffee could only mean one thing—Kyle. Harnessing his energy, Kit rolled to his side, pivoted to an upright position, and waited for the spinning in his head to stop before trying to stand up. The simple task of taking his tablets proved far more strenuous than he had anticipated. Once on his feet he reached for the coffee, holding it close to his nose. His senses made the necessary adjustments, and the warmth of the coffee provided a brief respite from the pounding in his head. Realizing he was still wearing much of the same clothing from the previous day, he headed toward the steam shower.

Dressed in a casual pair of blue jeans, a button-down shirt and loafers, Kit made his way from the master suite to the kitchen where he found Kyle sitting at the table reading the *New York Times*. "Good morning," Kyle said without putting the paper down.

"If you say so," Kit replied. "Why are you here?" Kit asked squinting his eyes as he spoke.

"I spoke to Sara and she asked me to look in on you so she wouldn't have to come in from the Hamptons," Kyle explained still holding the paper up in a reading position.

"Sweet of her to be so concerned," Kit said without hiding any of the intended sarcasm.

Kyle pulled the paper down and saw Kit's weary condition for the first time. "She does care for you just as I do," Kyle stated in a very matter-of-fact tone. Kit pulled out one of the barstools surrounding the 10-foot eating area. Sitting down and placing his head in his hands, it was clear Kit was still suffering from the effects of a monster hangover.

"You could use some food in your stomach. I am going to fix some breakfast. Eggs and bacon sound good?"

At the mention of food, Kit's stomach turned over. "Not really," Kit said never moving his head.

"I will fix plenty. You can eat something when you are up for it," Kyle said. With that Kyle was up looking for the supplies needed to prepare breakfast. Moments later the kitchen was filled with the smells of frying bacon. Normally, this smell would be enough to excite the senses of any man, but today the aroma brought nothing but nausea to the hungover man. Within minutes Kit had disappeared to find relief from his queasiness. Returning to the kitchen, Kit found Kyle waiting for him with a cold towel.

"Feel better?" Kyle asked with little sympathy.

"Surprisingly, yes," Kit responded with a hint a new energy in his voice. Taking the cold towel from Kyle and wiping his face, Kit made his way back onto the barstool.

Kyle had finished preparing breakfast and the bar now had a nice spread of eggs, bacon, and toast along with more fresh coffee. Kit hesitated for a moment then reached for a plate and added items to eat. Kyle had already filled his plate and was three bites into his eggs when Kit finally spoke. "Thank you."

Kyle stopped mid-bite to look up at Kit who was sitting motionless for those few seconds. "You are welcome," Kyle answered.

"Just one question: why?" Kit asked as he tried a bite of eggs.

"Kit, just because I don't agree with you and your tactics it does not mean I don't care for you as a person." Kit swallowed, looked at Kyle and asked, "So explain to me to me again why I feel as if I am being fired as a king?"

"I wondered how much you would remember from yesterday," Kyle said. "As I explained yesterday, I let you down by allowing you to become a king for the wrong reasons. A true king is purpose-centered and uses his gifts and talents to create a more meaningful life for those around them. Additionally, I wavered in my own principles and started displaying extended periods of situational integrity. In doing so I modeled for all my kings the wrong behaviors for being a king. It became okay to build your kingdoms for your own personal gain at the expense of everyone around you. I owed you better."

Kit finished his coffee, sat the cup on the bar, and asked, "Situational integrity?"

Kyle half smiled, "It simply means that a person's integrity can waver from a set of fixed principles depending on the situation."

At this point Kit's head hurt too badly to be upset or even put up a fight with Kyle. "So where do we go from here?" Kit asked as he poured more coffee, hoping the tablets he took earlier would kick in soon.

"For me, I have committed to creating new experiences by being purpose-centered, focused on a set of fixed principles to create a more meaningful life for those around me. That begins with Em," Kyle continued, "As for you and me, well, that somewhat depends on you. For most people, finding meaning in what they do is important to them. Most search their entire life for significance never finding what fulfills them. For a select few in the world, money, power and fame are used to fill the void. But even that select group eventually comes to realize that these are not sustainable. They find they are in a constant struggle to obtain more." Kit looked at Kyle without moving. He was indeed hanging on every word. No one other than Kyle Ellis would ever be able to speak to Kit in this manner. The king was being told he had no clothes. Kyle continued, "You have the opportunity to become a great king if you are willing to consider a new path. A path that is centered on purpose and fixed principles with the simple goal to create a more meaningful life for those you come in contact with in life. The question you need to consider is, are you all in?"

THE TOAST

Kyle and Emily stepped onto Central West, turned left and began their short, by City standards, walk to dinner. The City never sleeps and tonight was no different. A steady flow of cabs and pedestrians all made their way somewhere. For the first time in years, Emily wrapped her arm inside Kyle's as they walked in perfect stride. Kyle felt a warmth come over him that gave him a feeling of what some would call butterflies in his stomach. A feeling he had not felt in years. As they came to a stop at the corner of West 63rd to wait on a turning cab, Kyle leaned his head over and gave Emily a gentle kiss on top of her head. Emily squeezed Kyle's arm tighter as they continued their walk. For almost a dozen blocks no words were spoken although much had been communicated.

Once inside the restaurant Kyle helped Emily with her light jacket and they were seated in the upper section of the dining room affording them a splendid view of Columbus Circle. It was only after Kyle ordered the pre-dinner drinks that the conversation began. "Two glasses of the Tyler Pinot Noir?" Kyle said, glancing at Emily for final approval. The slight smile and nod from Emily was confirmation that he chose wisely.

Emily reached her hand across the table and placed it on Kyle's and said, "Should I forget later, thank you for a wonderful evening."

Kyle smiled, placing his other hand on Emily's. "You deserve a thousand more," Kyle said. "Em, I can't tell you how thankful I am for you. You have been very patient with me for longer than I deserve. I got off track. It took you, Mac, and Clara for me to see my blind spot. Thank you." Emily's heart began to race just a bit faster upon hearing vulnerability in the man she loved—a trait she found so very sexy in Kyle. She knew in her soul that true courage was not about the lack of fear but the willingness to face fear with vulnerability. Kyle's fear was his self-doubt. It drove him beyond the center point of his true purpose to a place where his decisions were made through a dubious lens—that of increasing his own kingdom at the extreme expense of others. Once Kyle accepted the reality of his situation, he made the choice to redirect his own path and take accountability for his destiny. That accountability began by refocusing his purpose in life and facing his past thoughts, feelings, and actions with the one he loved and trusted, Emily. Kyle decided to face the uncertainly of life with a centered purpose knowing now that he was worthy. This was true vulnerability. It was no longer about building a vast kingdom of powerful kings. Now it was about creating meaningful connections in life and that being enough.

Once their wine arrived Emily picked up her glass, swirled the wine a few times before speaking. "What should we toast to tonight?" she asked, tilting her glass toward Kyle.

"Second chances," he said without any hesitation.

Emily smiled, hanging her head slightly to one side. At this very moment all she could think about was wrapping her arms around her husband and burying her head deep into his chest. She knew that the man she fell in love with and married was back and her heart raced with joy. Leaning deeply into the table she reached her glass toward Kyle's, "Here's to second chances. May we give as many as we receive in life." Kyle grinned and gently touched glasses with Emily as if giving her a soft kiss.

THE TALK

Kyle: *"Downstairs"*

Mac: *"Everything OK?"*

Kyle: *"Out for a run…want to join?"*

Mac: *"Give me 5…want to come up?"*

Kyle: *"I'm good in lobby."*

Kyle was reading email on his phone when Mac stepped off the elevator. The sun had yet to make an appearance over the City. Just a few years ago, strolling the streets of Hells Kitchen at this hour of the morning would not have been encouraged. Even though the neighborhood surrounding Mac's 24-story high rise still required a high level of awareness, over the last decade a noticeable gentrification of the neighborhood had occurred, creating a haven for young professionals of the City. Over the years, Kyle had spent a considerable amount of time at Mac's place. The view of the skyline from the rooftop sky deck was second to none in the City. On more than one occasion the two friends enjoyed the guilty pleasure of a Montecristo Jacopo cigar while gazing down upon the energy of the City.

"Ready?" Mac said never breaking his stride toward the door. Kyle looked up from his phone to catch the back of Mac's head and began to follow behind. "You thinking a Park run or you want something more adventurous along the river?" Mac asked as the two men made their way to the sidewalk along West 52nd street.

"The Park. We can grab breakfast once we finish," responded Kyle. The two men quickly found a reasonable pace that took into consideration Kyle's recent heart troubles. They headed east toward 8th Avenue to find the city streets filled with trash bags from the night before, creating a makeshift obstacle course for the two runners. Once they reached 8th Avenue, they turned north toward Columbus Circle where they would enter the Park with its stream of early-morning runners. Mac understood from years of friendship with Kyle there was a specific agenda intended for this impromptu morning encounter. Knowing how to engage Kyle's agenda had taken Mac a few years to master, but he now understood the subtle nuances of Kyle's communication style. Letting Kyle own the dialogue, Mac learned, was the key. By the time the two had reached the traffic light at Columbus Circle, Kyle was ready to talk. Their breathing was noticeable as they stood facing the Park across the four lanes of West 59th Street. "Had dinner with Em at Per Se last night."

Mac made the immediate connection as he glanced to his left to see the location of the restaurant on Columbus Circle. "How was the experience?" Mac asked as the light gave clearance to proceed.

"Worth the trip, the food was every bite worth the price," Kyle offered.

"Not what I was asking," Mac said as the two entered the Park. Kyle showed a slight grin, appreciating the question from his friend. Mac knew Kyle only mentioned the dinner date to discuss his conversation with Emily and not the finer points of the culinary experience.

"It was one of our most enjoyable times together in years," Kyle exclaimed. "I shared my appreciation for her patience with me as I get back on track," Kyle confessed.

"So you were truly vulnerable with Em. How did that make you feel?" Mac asked.

"Thought I was going to have another heart attack at first. But when Em looked at me, I knew everything was going to be fine," Kyle explained as the two men turned onto Central Drive. "So what was your learning from the experience?" Mac asked.

"The power of the second chance should never be underestimated," Kyle exclaimed with no hesitation. Mac smiled at the words.

"Em offered a second chance to me with no hesitation, but only after I asked for it," Kyle continued.

"Do you think there is a connection between asking for a second chance and offering one?" Mac asked. Kyle's eyes narrowed as he considered Mac's question.

"Hadn't thought about it. Seems like there might be," Kyle replied. "Consider this: if Emily had approached you three weeks ago and said, 'I want to give you a second chance' what would have been your response?" Mac asked.

"Easy. Second chance for what?" Kyle said.

"Precisely. When there is no ownership for your current condition, second chances are meaningless," Mac explained. Kyle's head began to nod as he processed what Mac was saying. 'There must be an awareness of need before there can be an acceptance of help and healing," Mac finished.

Kyle halted to an immediate stop. After a couple of strides, Mac noticed Kyle was missing from his side. "You okay?" Mac said in a slightly elevated voice.

Kyle glanced at Mac and nodded the affirmative. "Just thinking about what you just said helps clear up some recent experiences. We are on the edge of a breakthrough with Kit but haven't been able to get him across the goal line," Kyle said.

"Kit will need to recognize his current path cannct fill the void he is feeling within his life. Until he comes to that conclusion, there can be no new life," Mac explained.

The two men were now at a casual strolling pace as they continued to talk. "The conversation with Michael might be more difficult than the one I had with Kit. At least Kit was receptive to the idea," Kyle said.

"What do you think makes Kit more receptive?" Mac asked.

"Reflecting back on our conversation I realize now that my vulnerability with Kit regarding my own skinned knees opened the door for a meaningful conversation," Kyle said.

Mac smiled at the revelation. "A simple principle of leadership is that your influence with others increases when you lead with love in place of judgment," Mac explained. "You were able to connect with Kit at an emotional level when he experienced your authentic love for him as a person. It is safe to assume many of Kit's encounters in life both personally and professionally have come out of a narrative of judgment from the cther person." Kyle nodded as he listened to the wisdom of his friend.

By this time in their outing, the two had arrived at the coffee and pastry shop in the center of the Park. "Coffee?" Kyle asked.

"Yes!" Mac answered in an enthusiastic voice. After picking up their coffee, the two continued their conversation as they walked through the Park. "Kyle, you need to understand what got you to the top of the game. You have a natural ability to see the strengths in others and build upon those strengths. You always have used your gift with a lens of true love for the other person. That is until a few years back. Something inside of you began to shift. It was a slow shift at first, but it picked up speed as time went on. Until here we are. As your friend I owed you better sooner," Mac said then took a drink of his coffee.

"I appreciate you, Mac, and all you have done for Emily and me over the years. You are a good friend," Kyle said with a soft and steady tone in his voice. Mac held his coffee up in the air in a toasting gesture and exclaimed, "Right back at you, my friend."

For the next several moments the two men walked in silence enjoying the beauty of the morning and the energy that springs to life inside the Park each day. When they arrived at West Drive waiting briefly to cross the street, Kyle broke the silence. "My meeting with Michael tomorrow will sound different after our talk this morning."

"What will be different?" Mac asked.

"First, my mindset going into the conversation is to lead with love, not judgment. Second, I am going to be vulnerable with him by sharing my own hardships."

Mac nodded in agreement, "That will be important for Michael. He always says that everything he learned about being a king came from you. What comes after vulnerability?"

"Well, I am going to focus on Michael's strengths," Kyle added.

Mac took a deep breath and said, "It's good to have the real Kingmaker back."

THE DECISION

By 8 a.m. the line of black private cars had begun to build in front of The Regency Bar & Grill on Park Avenue. Known for decades as the power breakfast go-to spot in the City, Kyle felt this venue would be the perfect place to face his fallen king. Being a Sunday morning Kyle had opted for a more casual attire of jeans, a custom-made shirt and jacket from his favorite tailor in SoHo. His choice of no socks and no tie this morning was of no surprise to Emily as she watched him get ready earlier.

The security threat surrounding Michael had diminished greatly over the last several weeks, thanks in large part to the work of Kyle's team, but Michael still felt the need for a nearby security detail. The Regency was no stranger to security given the number of power brokers that frequented the establishment. Kyle once joked that having breakfast at The Regency was like going to a king class reunion. Once inside Kyle found Michael sitting toward the back of the restaurant facing the front door, as instructed by his security team. As Kyle approached Michael, he noticed sitting one table in front of Michael was Todd Nelson, the former Secret Service agent hired to protect Michael. Dressed in a dark suit and sunglasses, Todd would not have seemed out of place in these surroundings and would most likely be easily mistaken for a famous star or Wall Street broker. It was the clear-colored ear piece draped over his left ear with the coiled wired running down the back of his neck disappearing into his suit jacket that was the instant giveaway. Had Kyle taken the time to study Todd's suit a bit closer, he would have noticed the slight bulge on his left side, the telltale sign of his Sig Sauer P228, a holdover from his days in the Secret Service. Giving a pleasant nod to Todd as he passed, Kyle knew not to expect any response in return.

Michael pushed the beige armchair back to stand and greet his old friend the Kingmaker. Kyle had always appreciated the deliberately firm handshake from Michael. The two men exchanged warm greetings then sat down to enjoy one of the best breakfasts in the City. Anticipating Kyle's order Michael had a fresh cup of coffee waiting for Kyle when he arrived.

"How is Mackenzie?" Kyle asked to begin the conversation.

"She misses Emily. Other than that she is fine. Just returned from the Malibu house last night. She was still asleep when I left the apartment this morning," Michael said. "We should get the girls together and have drinks later today," Kyle offered as he glanced at the menu.

"Brilliant idea," Michael exclaimed as he began to text Mackenzie the idea. Within minutes Michael's phone gave a light buzz indicating a text message. "Guess Kenz is up," Michael said with a slight smile. After reading the text message Michael proclaimed, "Looks like we are on for drinks. Our place, say 7:00?"

Kyle was well into his text to Emily once he heard the news and almost instantly she replied. "Seven will be perfect. Now, how about some breakfast?"

It had been several days since Michael and Kyle had spoken, but this morning seemed like they hadn't seen or heard from each other for months. The conversation flowed very naturally on both of their parts. Michael's gratitude for the work Kyle had done was outwardly apparent in every part of the conversation. Kyle made a deliberate point to lead with love by expressing his sincere appreciation for Michael as a person. The conversation had developed to just the right point for Kyle to share with Michael as he had with Kit. "In reflecting back to our conversation at the Lazy Deuce, I realize I owe you an apology," Kyle began.

"Nonsense! There were a host of things said that night that neither one of us should be held accountable for. It was an exceptionally difficult time," Michael responded.

"I understand," Kyle offered quickly. "However, there was one moment that has stuck with me. Bottom line, I owe you an apology and a thank you," Kyle continued.

"Okay, now you are going to have to fill me in on what you are talking about," Michael said with a growing puzzled look on his face.

"You commented to me all you have learned about being a king you learned from me," Kyle said with a slight matter-of-fact tone to his voice.

"I remember," Michael replied.

"Well, truth be told Michael, I owe you better," Kyle said, never breaking eye contact with Michael.

"Owe me better," Michael exclaimed in a voice loud enough to cause Todd to glace around to ensure everyone was okay. "Owe me better. What are you thinking? You just saved me from potentially the largest corporate disaster of my career. You don't owe me anything," Michael said with a stern tone.

"Michael, I realized that I have lost my way and have drifted from my true purpose in life. By doing so I modeled for you the wrong behavior for being a king. You helped me see that and I am grateful to you." Michael sat quietly for a moment as he collected his thoughts on what he just heard from Kyle. After all these years to hear the Kingmaker admit he was wrong created a revelation he had not prepared himself for. As one of the most feared players on Wall Street, Michael Allan rarely found himself caught off guard, especially when it came to people. Additionally, Michael had no current ability to process the vulnerability Kyle was demonstrating. The difficulty for Michael at this moment was his current definition of vulnerability equated to weakness. There had been numerous individuals over the years when showing signs of vulnerability would end up another victim of a Prime Networks takeover. For Michael, this moment was complicated.

The server cleared the remaining plates from the table as the two men sat in semi-silence. Kyle offered the first real conversation in what seemed like an eternity. "When I made the decision to get into this business, it was never to become a kingmaker. I found myself with a unique skill and a passion for helping others reach their full potential in life. I was centered on my purpose and driven daily by a set of fixed principles. My intention in life was to make a positive impact on those I encountered. Along the way I experienced what worldly power felt like. With each experience I grew to crave more power and all that comes with it. I had no idea the grip worldly power had on me. The grip was so strong it moved me off the foundation of my fixed principles into a place of situational integrity. Michael, I was outside my purpose center and growing more addicted each day to the controlling demands of worldly power. I was defenseless to my addiction and could not see the impact it was having on my life and the life of those around me. The false story of my life created unlimited experiences, which wrongly validated my actions as truth. I owe you better." Michael's face began to lose color as he sat motionless listening to Kyle. For 90 seconds every word Kyle spoke rang loudly in Michael's ears. How was he to process what he was hearing from his friend? There was a decision needed and for the first time in his adult life, Michael Allan was unable to determine how to proceed.

THE DOOR

Mac pulled along the Upper East Side Park Avenue curb just before 7 p.m. The impromptu gathering of the Ellises and Allans was about to take place. The very polished doorman greeted the Mercedes sedan and with a well-rehearsed fluid motion opened the door and greeted Kyle. "Good evening, Mr. Ellis. It is wonderful to see you again." Upon helping Emily out of the car, the doorman effortlessly stepped under the green canopy to assist with the front door. The doors to the building were made of solid brass fashioned in an impressive art deco design. Fitting for the pre-war building that stood at this Park Avenue corner known to most as the home of billionaires. The white-gloved doorman pulled the massive door open to reveal a space few in the City had ever seen. "Enjoy your evening."

Upon exiting the private elevator Kyle and Emily were immediately greeted by the strikingly beautiful Mackenzie Allan. At 5' 9" Mackenzie was naturally tall. Tonight, in her high heels, her power shoes as she like to call them, she was an imposing figure able to look in the eye of most everyone in the room that evening. The simple, yet elegant couture black cocktail dress Mackenzie wore had a low plunging back with a simple drop front. The dress was perfectly accented by a strand of Tiffany Akoya cultured pearls that lay delicately across her neck. Her long dark hair flowed effortlessly past her shoulders as she happily greeted Emily at the elevator. Instantly they embraced, standing for several moments just enjoying being in each other's presence.

"You look stunning this evening," Kyle said as he stole a kiss on the cheek from Mackenzie.

"A far cry from the last time we saw each other," Mackenzie replied with a hint of amusement in her voice.

Michael appeared from the adjacent hallway to greet his guests. Always dressed for business, tonight was a simpler affair for Michael. Casually dressed with no tie and a sport coat, Michael presented a presence of power even though it was just an evening of drinks with friends. Stepping forward to kiss Emily on the cheek, he exclaimed, "Welcome. It has been too long since we have had the two of you over. Come in." Michael extended his right hand to Kyle while placing his left hand on Kyle's shoulder, gently squeezing as a way of showing his extreme gratitude that the Kingmaker was in his home.

The couples made their way into the gallery of the Park Avenue townhome. Once they were in the area of the home filled with fine artwork, they were greeted by two staff holding trays of light hors d'oeuvres. The gallery of the home had 10-foot ceilings with museum-quality lights. The walls were covered with various genres of art collected mostly by Mackenzie over the last several years. The couples admired the latest addition to the collection, an obscure impressionist painting of a man in top hat, black top-coat, walking stick and white scarf draped around his neck. The man in the painting was standing on a sidewalk looking toward a large 18th century building facing two separate, oversized, hand-carved wooden doors. Mackenzie's face glowed as she talked about her latest purchase from a gallery in Los Angeles.

"What can I offer you to drink, Em?" Mackenzie asked.

"Wine would be wonderful," Emily responded as the two ladies retreated to the wood paneled library where the entrance into the wine cellar was located. For a brief moment Kyle and Michael remained in the gallery positioned in front of Mackenzie's latest purchase.

"The noteworthy thing about this picture is the name," Michael offered as Kyle studied the painting closer.

"Why is that?" Kyle asked not taking his eyes from the work studying each brush stroke.

"The painting is named 'Decisions,'" proclaimed Michael with a slight grin.

Kyle turned from the painting to face Michael with a look that signaled to Michael that more explanation was needed. "Come on, let me get you a drink and I will tell you what I mean," Michael said as he placed his arm on Kyle's shoulder to guide him to the library.

By the time the men arrived, the ladies had discovered the perfect wine for the evening, a Soter Vineyard White Label Pinot Noir. As they retreated to the main living room, where they met with breathtaking views of the City, the men made their way to the bar.

"What will it be?" Michael asked, pulling two glasses from the lighted shelf. Kyle grinned as he remembered the last time a king poured himself a drink.

"Scotch."

Michael opened the leaded-glass door to produce a clear bottle with amber colored liquid. The label on the bottle read, Highland Park Single Malt Scotch Whiskey, aged 30 years. "I've been looking for a good reason to open this bottle," Michael explained as he gave the cap a twist to break the seal. "Ice?" Michael asked.

"I'm good without, thank you," Kyle replied.

Michael handed Kyle his drink while extending his in the air to present a toast. "To Kings and Queens."

Kyle lifted his glass, smiled and took a sip of the 30-year-old scotch. The smooth sweet favor followed by a delicate hint of smoke brought a relaxed smile to his face.

"Magnificent," Kyle exclaimed.

"It is tough to beat a 30-year scotch from Scotland," Michael said after taking his first sample of the drink. Motioning to the seating area, Michael led the way for the two men to sit and talk.

The low-back, art deco leather chairs were the perfect sanctuary from the day. A small fire in the fireplace created the perfect ambiance.

"Kenz has asked that we not smoke cigars in the apartment," Michael said.

"No problem. This scotch is fine without one," Kyle replied. "I'm still thinking about the painting and your comment earlier," Kyle continued. "What makes the title so noteworthy?"

Michael took another sip of his drink, paused and responded, "I left breakfast this morning feeling as though there was a decision I needed to make."

"What decision?" Kyle asked having a general idea of what Michael may have been struggling with.

"Hearing your story caused me to re-think my own life. I must admit, today has been a very contemplative day. Even Kenz asked about me," Michael explained.

"What have you been contemplating?" Kyle asked.

"Listening to you was similar to listening to myself. Kyle, I am a product of you, only worse," Michael said, finishing off his drink. Rising out of his chair Michael walked to the bar and poured himself another drink. With the bottle in his hand, he motioned toward Kyle for a refresh.

Kyle lifted his hand to indicate he was good with his drink at that moment. Kyle knew Michael had reached a critical point in his awareness of his life. "So what did you decide?" Kyle asked.

"I appreciate you sharing your story with me, but that is your story not mine." With that Michael took a long draw on his fresh drink.

Kyle sat quietly as he processed what Michael was saying. "What would you say your story is, Michael?" Kyle asked

"My story is just being written, Kyle. There is so much more to do and nothing is going to stop me now. Not some thug gang of Russians, not you, my father, or Mackenzie." Michael said as he paced the room, his voice slightly elevated.

Michael's words brought shivers over Kyle's body. "What do you mean by 'not Mackenzie?'" Kyle asked not wanting to hear the answer.

"I am certain Kenz has confided in Emily by now that we are getting a divorce," Michael said, now at a complete stop standing directly in front of the window.

Kyle could feel his heart skip a beat in his chest as he listened to the news from Michael. "Michael, I am sorry to hear that," Kyle offered

"Look, it was bound to happen. We have grown apart. The security scare was the tipping point. She browbeat me after you left the ranch that day to change my ways. She told me I was being unfair to you and I owed you better. Funny, she even mentioned I was addicted to power."

Kyle's face was wrenched with emotion as he continued to listen to Michael tell his story. As he sat searching for the right words, he heard the soft whispered voice of Emily from the doorway.

"Kyle, I am sorry to interrupt, but I am having Mac take Kenz and me back to our place," Emily said as she stood just outside of the sightline of the Michael who was still looking out the window. Kyle turned to face Emily and with a nod agreed that he understood why.

Without turning around from the window, Michael spoke, "Thanks, Em. You're a good friend to Kenz."

Emily's eyes showed a deep sadness as she turned from the door to go comfort her dear friend. She knew the next few days would be difficult and that Mackenzie would need her.

The two men remained in silence for several minutes as the enormity of the situation sank in. Michael had made his decision, he had chosen his door in life and it would be to remain on the path of worldly power fueled by his pride, destined to self-destruct at some point in the future. Kyle knew that it was not a matter of *if*, but a matter of *when*. In a final effort to redirect Michael from future ruin, Kyle made one last plea.

"Michael, we have known each other for many years. You have a unique set of skills that set you apart from all others in the marketplace. I have seen you use these strengths to better mankind and the results have been extraordinary. Refocusing your purpose could make use of your skills and talents to change the world for generations to come. Isn't that the legacy you want to leave?"

Michael sat his drink on the window ledge and turned toward his old friend. "Kyle, the only person I care to worry about at this moment is myself. And with your help, we can build a kingdom so powerful that people will shudder when I walk into a room.

That's the legacy I want to build. Together we are unstoppable. All other kings will pale in my shadow."

Michael's words tore through Kyle, but not nearly as bad as the outcome of the evening. Kyle began, "Michael, I am afraid this is one journey you are going to go on alone. We are done." And with that Kyle rose to his feet, placed his glass on the side table, and turned toward the door.

"Don't be a fool, Kyle," Michael roared from the other side of the room. "You are in this too deep to get out. You made me and you are just like me," Michael continued.

Kyle stopped just before he reached the door, turning one last time toward the king he had created. "Part of what you say may be true. I did make you, but not for this. I was like you, but I have chosen a new door in life and the offer is still open for you to join me."

Michael watched as the one who helped guide his life from nothing to one of the most powerful players on Wall Street stood ready to walk out of his life. Michael simply turned his back on Kyle to stare out the window onto the City lights. "Give my best to Em." And with that the king had fallen one final time.

***

Kyle: *"You close by?"*

Mac: *"Dropping off Em and Kenz now."*

Kyle: *"Pick me up at 65th and 5th."*

Mac: *"Heard."*

Kyle exited Michael's building onto Park Avenue and began walking toward 65th Street. The last moments of his conversation with Michael were still playing in his head. He was devastated by the decisions Michael had made and for those who would eventually end up in his path of destruction – especially Mackenzie.

Kyle: *"How are you?"*

Emily: *"I am fine. Kenz is a wreck. I suspected something was up when we arrived."*

Kyle: *"How?"*

Emily: *"Girl intuition."*

Kyle: *"I will hang with Mac tonight to give you two some time."*

Emily: *"So thoughtful. I love having you back! How are you?"*

Kyle: *"Deeply hurt. Michael chose to stay on his current path."*

Emily: *"So very sorry."*

Kyle: *"Love you."*

Emily: *"Love you, too."*

Kyle had made the turn on 65th to walk the two blocks to 5th Avenue where Mac would pick him up. Within minutes Kyle was standing at the crosswalk waiting for the light to clear him to cross to the other side of 5th. Mac had timed his arrival perfectly and was waiting curbside.

Stepping inside the car Kyle saw a small package on the seat next to his. The bag had a familiar logo on the side, Davidoff of Geneva, one of the City's top cigar shops.

"Stopped by to pick up a couple of your favorites. Thought we could stare at the City from the rooftop terrace tonight," Mac said never taking his eyes off the road.

Kyle smiled as he picked up the bag and peered inside – two Montecristo Jacopo cigars; Mac knew just what was needed. As they headed toward Mac's apartment there was no need for words. The two rode in silence, processing the day's events. It was moments like these when Kyle fully appreciated having Mac in his life.

THE CITY

On the 24th floor terrace Mac and Kyle pulled up two teakwood lounge chairs to face the downtown view of the City. From the rooftop of Mac's building, the City was perfectly framed from the Empire State to Central Park looking west from 10th Avenue. The City lights were a perfect contrast against the deep blue cloudless sky. On the 24th floor the sounds of the City were dampened but never completely disappeared. There was a magnificent energy to the great City.

From his jacket pocket Kyle produced the two finely wrapped sticks waiting to be lit. Mac's liquor cabinet was a far cry from that of Michael Allan's so Kyle happily settled for a cold beer to accompany his $50 cigar.

The soft glow of the tip of Kyle's cigar indicated the beginning of the end of a challenging day. The distant and ever-present high pitch of a fire truck making its way through the busy streets of the City was the only discernable sound for several moments as the two men enjoyed the rare pleasure of a fine cigar.

"Michael chose to stay on his current path," Mac opened with a somewhat matter-of-fact tone.

"That is putting it lightly. Not only did he choose to not change his course, he did it in a extremely defiant way," Kyle noted. "Pushing out Mackenzie was uncalled for. I didn't see that coming."

"What do you suppose was the tipping point for Michael?" Mac asked.

"Easy. Pride," Kyle offered. "He also mentioned his father. Michael hasn't spoken to me about his father for more than 10 years. Michael once shared with me that his father placed tremendous shame on him for failing early in his career."

"Interesting. How do your observations connect with all that you have learned over the last several weeks?" Mac asked taking a long draw on his now-lit cigar.

Kyle stared into the City lights as he pondered Mac's question. "It seems when your purpose in life is centered on yourself, it produces self-pride. When you are driven by self-pride, situational integrity increases. A fall is inevitable," Kyle said. "I would add that Michael was uncomfortable with my demonstrating vulnerability. He made me believe vulnerability was a weakness and therefore something to be avoided. Thinking like that may have come from his father. I can't imagine the shame Michael is carrying around from the years he spent working for his dad."

"Shame is a debilitating emotion," Mac stated with a sympathetic tone. "I first encountered the impact of shame while working on my Doctorate," Mac continued. "The impact on a person's life can be devastating if not dealt with appropriately," Mac said shaking his head as he recalled the numerous people he worked with during his final years of school. "My experience has taught me people can develop some type of addiction over time to numb the toxic pain they feel from the hurt of shame. Based on your time with Michael, did he demonstrate any signs of addiction?" Mac asked.

Kyle pondered the question deeply before answering, "It seemed as though the accumulation of power was Michael's drug of choice to numb his feelings of shame. He mentioned his desire for a kingdom so powerful others shuddered when he walked into the room," he recalled.

"Power is a seductive drug that is not easy to walk away from once you have a taste. Clearly, for Michael it's been more than a taste," Mac added.

"Mac, you know that I have felt the relentless pull of worldly power in my own life. It seems the farther away from my purpose center, I became more self-absorbed in my own kingdom I became. Now, I can see that very thing happening to Michael," Kyle said.

"So where do you go from here with Michael?" Mac asked.

"I told him we could no longer work together," Kyle said before he took a long drink from his bottle.

"What are your thoughts about that?" Mac asked.

"Broke my heart," Kyle responded while staring into the City. "I want to help him and will be here if he wants to change his direction, but I can no longer be an enabler to his behavior."

"I know how difficult that had to be for you. You need to know that was the right thing to do. I'm proud of you," Mac said.

Kyle took another puff of his cigar and replied, "That means a great deal. Thank you, my friend."

THE CHAIR

The last time Kyle was in Kit's office, Kit was demolishing a $10,000 bottle of scotch on his way to a world-class hangover. But it also brought with it Kit's willingness to hear Kyle out as he challenged Kit to change his current path.

"Thank you for coming by on short notice," Kit began.

"My pleasure, Kit. What's on your mind?" Kyle asked.

"Our talk," Kit said. "You asked me to consider if I was willing to be 'all in.' I haven't been able to get your question out of my head."

Kit made his way from behind his expansive desk to formally greet Kyle. "I would offer you a drink, but I have given up drinking for a while," Kit said with a wry smile.

"I'm good, thanks," Kyle replied.

Kit motioned to Kyle to have a seat in one of two high-back wing chairs in the seating area of his office. "I have to tell you how much I appreciate what you did for me last week. Outside of Sara, you are my last friend now that Howard is gone," Kit said with a serious look on his face. When Sara returned from the Hamptons, we had a long talk and she reminded me of how I got to where I am today."

Kyle listened intently as Kit began to transform before him. "How do you want to define success in the future?" Kyle asked.

"I am not going to lie, Kyle. I've been struggling with this. For so many years success has been about power and money. When you shared your story with me, at first I thought you were just weak. But the more I considered what you shared, I began to realize how much courage it took to do so," Kit said.

"Thank you for saying that," Kyle replied.

"I need help in understanding a different definition of success," Kit said.

"Kit, I shared with you that I owed you better. That begins with helping you find true success. Based on what I have learned, true success is linked to being purpose-centered. We need to identify your purpose in life. Then we will discuss a set of fixed principles from which you will conduct your business. These principles will be non-negotiable in how you conduct your business," Kyle offered.

"So far, I am with you. I've been giving this some thought. But all in? Help me understand this." Kit said.

Kyle took a moment to collect his thoughts. Getting up he walked to place himself directly behind his chair. "Kit, think of it this way. You have two chairs in life to choose from. One choice is the majestic throne of a king in which people are put in place to serve the king. The other choice is the humble chair of a king who serves his people in order to make them stronger. The first king focuses on the hands and feet of his people, getting them to do as he demands. The second king is focused on the hearts and minds of his people, which connect at an emotional level driving them to do all you need and more. The all-in king is purpose-centered, with fixed principles leading from a chair of humility." Kyle paused to let Kit mentally catch up.

After a brief moment Kyle looked at Kit and asked, "There is much to process. You need to know I will be with you the entire way. I just need to know if you are in."

Kit rose to his feet and walking toward Kyle, extended his hand, his eyes moist from tears. With a firm grip of Kyle's hand, Kit said, "I'm in!"

LEARNING POINTS:
THE KINGMAKER

1. Purpose-centered: Living by a set of fixed principles pursuing your passion, leveraging your strength, discerning your why, while making a positive difference with others.

2. Success: When purpose, talent, and resources come together to meet the needs of others.

3. Situational integrity: Allowing your integrity, living your life with honesty and a fixed set of moral principles, to shift based on the situation you are in with the sole intent to get what you desire.

4. Blind spots: Potentially destructive areas in our life we can not see due to lack of outside mentoring and feedback.

5. Simple principle of leadership: Your influence with others increases when you lead with love, demonstrate vulnerability, and focus on your strengths.

6. The power of second chances: We should give as many "second chances" as we receive, but realize when there is no ownership for one's circumstances, second chances are meaningless.

7. The Kingmaker: Leads by serving. Is focused on unlocking purpose-centered potential in others.

ACKNOWLEDGMENTS

Now that the manuscript is done, it is time to write the needed additional pages for the book to be complete. Second, after the Dedication is the Acknowledgments page, which, after doing my prep work, I realized is my personal list of kingmakers.

If a kingmaker is someone who sees potential in you, focuses on your strengths, and helps you rise above your circumstances in life, then my life is filled with those people. To begin the list is my beautiful bride of 25 years, Dee. Always a supporter, a friend, and one who helps me find my blind spots.

To bring any book to life requires an army of talent focused on the success of others. Leading the army, from my new publisher, Elevate Publishing, is Mark Russell who saw potential and has leaned into my strength. Additionally, my new editor, Anna McHargue, is a blessing and a true kingmaker in every sense. Daniel Morris, Dr. Joe Cook, and Dr. Brent Taylor are constant sounding boards to the never ceasing stream of energy I seem to display. To Kelli Valade, you have inspired me as a true purpose-centered leader since we met. I am grateful for your example. Leanne Folse, my amazing assistant, whose superpower is her ability to keep me focused and on task, is a true partner.

Looking over my journal notes I realize that if I listed all the other people in my life who have helped unlock my potential, the pages of acknowledgments would rival the pages in the book. My passion in life to help others find and unlock their purpose is fueled by the love shown to me by so many in the course of my lifetime.

In my first book I referenced the notion of a standard acknowledgment clause that should show up in every acknowledgment written, "To those I may have forgotten, thank you." More than ever, this statement is true for this work.

It should also be acknowledged this book serves as a daily reminder to me to live my life in a way that is purposed-centered and focused on the success of others. My hope and prayer to the reader is that these pages offer renewed encouragement to discover the true power of your purpose in life.

Onward!

TONY BRIDWELL

As an author, international speaker, consultant and coach, Tony Bridwell has been making a difference at some of the world's largest organizations for the past 20 years. He is the former Chief People Officer of Brinker International and a current partner with global consulting firm, Partners In Leadership.

Tony is a highly recognized thought leader in corporate culture, L&D, and human resources, being named 2015 HR Executive of the Year by DallasHR (the local SHRM affiliate) and also receiving the 2015 Strategic Leadership Award from Strategic Excellence HR.

Tony has been a facilitator and featured speaker for audiences of several thousand people and has presented for multiple conferences and associations, including the CHRO Exchange, Dallas

HR (SHRM), the HRSouthwest Conference, ATD San Diego, and the California Restaurant Association. Tony is also a member of SHRM and serves on the board of directors for Unlimited Partnerships and Taylor's Gift Foundation.

When he is not spending time with his family, Tony turns his efforts toward mentoring a small group of young men, cycling and writing. With three grown children and two dogs, Tony and his wife, Dee, have called the Dallas area home for almost 30 years.

AUTHOR'S RELATED WORK

Available on

elevate
publishing

A strategic publisher empowering authors to strengthen their brand.

Visit Elevate Publishing for our latest offerings.
www.elevatepub.com

NO TREES WERE HARMED
IN THE MAKING OF THIS BOOK

OK, so a few did need to make
the ultimate sacrifice.

In order to steward our environment,
we are partnering with *Plant With Purpose*, to plant
a tree for every tree that paid the price for the printing of
this book.

PLANT WITH PURPOSE

www.plantwithpurpose.org

go to www.elevatepub.com/about to learn more